Start Your Own

FREIGHT BROKERAGE BUSINESS

WITHDRAWAL

D1089336

Additional titles in *Entrepreneur's* **Startup Series**

Start Your Own

Entrepreneur
MAGAZINE'S

start*up*

Start Your Own

2nd EDITION

FREIGHT BROKERAGE BUSINESS

Your Step-by-Step Guide to Success

Entrepreneur Press and Jacquelyn Lynn

Ep
Entrepreneur
Press

Editorial Director: Jere L. Calmes
Managing Editor: Marla Markman
Cover Design: Beth Hansen-Winter
Production and composition: Eliot House Productions

This publication is designed to provide accurate and authoritative information in regard to the subject matter covered. It is sold with the understanding that the publisher is not engaged in rendering legal, accounting or other professional services. If legal advice or other expert assistance is required, the services of a competent professional person should be sought.

Library of Congress Cataloging-in-Publication Data
Lynn, Jacquelyn.
    Start your own freight brokerage business/by Entrepreneur Press and Jacquelyn Lynn.—2nd ed.
      p.   cm.
    Rev ed. of: Start your own freight brokerage business, 2003.
    Includes index.
    ISBN 1-932531-97-1 (9781932531978: alk. paper)
    ISBN 978-1-932531-97-8
      1. Freight and freightage. 2. New business enterprises. I. Lynn, Jacquelyn. Start your own freight brokerage business. II. Entrepreneur Press. III. Title.

    HE199.A2L96 2006
    388'.0440681—dc22   2006002673

Printed in Canada

12 11 10 09 08 07   10 9 8 7 6 5 4 3 2

Contents

▲

Preface

Ever been set up on a blind date by a friend? If you have—whether it was a success or a disaster—you've essentially seen a broker in operation.

The role of a broker is to bring two parties together. That might be in a social setting, such as the matchmaker who introduces a single man to a single woman. Or it might be in a business setting, such as a real estate broker who brings buyers and sellers together, a stock broker who brings investors and companies together, or a freight broker who brings shippers and carriers together.

Of course, when your Great Aunt Agnes wants to introduce you to that "perfect" person, the only reward she's hoping for is the satisfaction of being the catalyst behind a successful relationship—and perhaps some recognition at the wedding. But in business, brokers expect to be compensated for their matchmaking efforts, and justifiably so. They perform an extremely valuable service, bringing together buyers and sellers who might not otherwise be able to find each other and assisting in negotiating the terms of the transaction.

Brokers in passenger transportation are typically known as travel agents. Their function is to identify and arrange the most appropriate travel methods for their clients, whether it's booking a single, one-way seat on an airplane or putting together an elaborate tour package that includes surface and air passage, hotels, meals and recreation.

On the freight side of the transportation industry, the primary role of a broker is to help companies that need to ship cargo find a trucking company that can deliver the shipment on time and in good condition and provide any extra services that may be required—all at a competitive price.

Why can't shippers just do this for themselves? Simply put, because it isn't practical or realistic for them to be intimately familiar with the service and rate structures of hundreds of different motor freight companies. Even if they build in the cost of the broker's commission—which the carrier, not the shipper, often pays—most shippers save money and receive better service by using a freight broker rather than shopping around for freight services on their own. It's similar to using a travel agent; although many people think it costs more to use one, it's often cheaper to go through a middleman (travel agent, broker, or otherwise) than it is to make transactions directly.

From the carrier's perspective, the broker brings in business that the carrier might not have been able to find on its own. Unlike an in-house salesperson, the broker is only paid when the carrier hauls a load. Carriers respect and appreciate the role brokers play in keeping the transportation industry moving.

Of course, there's much more to the process than making an introduction and collecting a commission. Brokers work hard in a fast-paced, demanding environment. They thrive on stress, enjoy challenges, and are consummate "people" people. If your ideal business includes a predictable routine and a limited amount of human contact, stop reading right now, because a freight brokerage isn't for you. But if you want minute-by-minute change, unexpected crises, and daily opportunities to stretch your creativity and problem-solving abilities to the maximum, you'll make a great freight broker.

This book will take you through the process of starting a freight brokerage, beginning with a general overview of the freight industry and the role brokers play. It will explain basic requirements and start-up costs. You'll learn about day-to-day operations when things are going well—and when they're going wrong. We'll discuss how to find, hire and keep good employees—as well as what to do when you lose them. You'll gain a solid understanding of the sales and marketing process, as well as how to track and manage the financial side of your business. Throughout the book, you'll hear from freight brokers who have built successful companies and are eager to share what they learned.

Ready? Then turn the page to take the next step of your journey into one of the most fundamentally necessary and exciting businesses in the world: the freight brokerage.

1

Introduction
to the Freight
Brokerage Business

The transportation industry in general, and the trucking industry specifically, are critical to the economic and social survival of local communities, the country, and, indeed, the entire world. Think about the times major transportation systems have failed because of mechanical problems, natural disasters, or labor conflicts. When cargo can't move, the repercussions are serious and widespread. Store shelves are emptied, perishable goods spoil, factories are shut down, workers are idled—the list goes on.

The United States may be shifting from a manufacturing to an information-based economy, and technology is certainly impacting every business, but there will never be a time when goods do not have to move.

"Logistics professionals in the United States—shippers, intermediaries, and carriers—have transformed the way we do business," says Robert A. Voltmann, executive director and CEO of the Transportation Intermediaries Association (TIA) in Alexandria, Virginia. "In the process, our national economy has been transformed as well. Transportation has become a strategic asset. Inventory is now stored in motion as we have been able to move to just-in-time delivery. More goods are being moved and with more efficiency and reliability than ever before."

Take a look around your home or office. It's highly unlikely that you have much—if anything at all—that didn't reach you either entirely or partially by truck. The size and scope of the motor freight industry can be overwhelming. The good news is that there's plenty of room for you to start and grow a profitable business serving the industry as a freight broker.

What exactly is a freight broker? Very simply, it is an individual or a company that brings together a shipper that needs to transport goods with an authorized motor carrier that wants to provide the service. The legal definitions of "broker" and "brokerage service" are found in the Code of Federal Regulations, 49CFR371.3:

> *Broker means a person who, for compensation, arranges or offers to arrange the transportation of property by an authorized motor carrier. Motor carriers, or persons who are employees or bona fide agents of carriers, are not brokers within the meaning of this section when they arrange or offer to arrange the transportation of shipments which they are authorized to transport and which they have accepted and legally bound themselves to transport.*

> *Brokerage or brokerage service is the arranging of transportation or the physical movement of a motor vehicle or of property. It can be performed on behalf of a motor carrier, consignor or consignee. Nonbrokerage service is all other service performed by a broker on behalf of a motor carrier, consignor or consignee.*

A freight broker falls into the category of transportation intermediary, which is a company that is neither a shipper nor an asset-owning carrier, but plays a role in the movement of cargo. "Transportation intermediaries leverage their knowledge, investment in technology, and people resources to help both the shipper and carrier succeed," says Voltmann.

Fun Fact

According to a recent survey in *Transportation Journal* magazine, the aspects brokers enjoy most about their work are solving problems for customers and the fast-paced environment. What do they find most frustrating? The lack of trucks, and the feeling that brokers are not respected as professionals.

Brokers provide an important and valuable service to both motor carriers and shippers. They help carriers fill their trucks and earn a commission for their efforts. They help shippers find reliable motor carriers that they (the shippers) might not have otherwise known about. In fact, some companies use brokers as their traffic department, allowing the broker to coordinate all their shipping needs.

Brokers are not new to the trucking industry; they've been around since the industry itself began in the early part of the 20th century. Prior to the 1970s, however, regulations governing brokers were so restrictive that few firms were willing to even try to gain entry into the industry. But with dramatic changes in federal transportation policy during the 1970s, regulatory restrictions have been eased, creating new entrepreneurial opportunities in the third-party logistics arena.

The Players

An industry so huge and diverse requires a wide range of participants to thrive. Some of these participants' titles may be a bit confusing, and some of their responsibilities may overlap. But to keep things clear and as simple as possible, let's look at who the key players are and what they do.

- *Freight broker.* A freight broker is the middleman who connects shippers and carriers. Freight brokers are also known as "truck brokers," "transportation brokers," and "property brokers." Though we will consistently use the term "freight broker" in this book, you may see or hear these other titles elsewhere.

- *Shipper.* A shipper is an entity that has products or goods to transport. Technically, shippers can be individuals or companies, but as a broker, you will deal most often with businesses in manufacturing or agriculture industries.

- *Motor carrier.* A motor carrier is a company that provides truck transportation. There are two types of motor carriers: private (a company that provides truck transportation of its own cargo), and for hire (a company that is paid to provide truck transportation of cargo belonging to others). There are two types of for-hire carriers: common and contract. A common carrier serves the public under two stringent obligations: compulsory service and liability for loss or damage to goods. A contract carrier transports freight under contract with one or a limited number of shippers.

Smart Tip

Many shippers who have their own fleets (private carriers) occasionally function as contract carriers. Many of their trips are one way, and they often work with brokers to find loads to carry on their return trips. Build relationships with private carriers whenever you can.

3

▲

- *Freight forwarder.* Often confused with freight brokers, freight forwarders are significantly different. Forwarders typically take possession of the goods, consolidate numerous smaller shipments into one large shipment, then arrange for transport of that larger shipment. To transport goods, surface freight forwarders use both motor freight and rail carriage; air freight forwarders use cargo and passenger airlines; and ocean freight forwarders use water carriers.

- *Import-export broker.* These people are facilitators for importers and exporters (import brokers are also referred to as customhouse brokers). Import-export brokers interface with U.S. Customs, other government agencies, international carriers, and other companies and organizations that are involved in international freight transportation.

- *Agricultural truck broker.* Generally small and operating in one area of the country, unregulated agricultural truck brokers arrange motor carrier service for exempt agricultural products.

- *Shippers associations.* Shippers associations are exempt, nonprofit, cooperative organizations formed by shippers to reduce transportation costs by pooling shipments. Shippers associations operate in a manner very similar to that of freight forwarders, but their services are limited to their members and are not available to the general public. Since trucking deregulation in the 1970s, the number of shippers associations has declined significantly.

In a perfect world, of course, each entity in the industry would handle its traditional role and that's all. However, the transportation industry is changing so rapidly that

---

A Truck by any other Name

The term "truck" is an umbrella word covering a wide range of equipment. Among the types of trucks you'll need to be familiar with are:

- ○ Dry vans (nonrefrigerated semitrailers)
- ○ Refrigerated semitrailers (or "reefers")
- ○ Flats or flatbeds (flat trailers built to handle heavy loads such as metal and machinery)
- ○ Liquid tankers (trailers designed to carry liquid or fine bulk materials)
- ○ Ragtops (canvas-covered, boxlike trailers)
- ○ Containers (shipping containers used for freight carried on ships or trains)
- ○ Air-ride (trailers built to reduce road shock and designed to carry fragile items)

---

once-distinctive lines are blurring. Also, it's quite common for a successful freight broker to expand his or her business by creating subsidiaries or additional companies that offer other freight services.

A key issue, say industry experts, is that legal definitions have not been challenged recently, so freight forwarders may be acting as brokers and brokers may assume the role of freight forwarders. In the event of a cargo claim or nonpayment of bills, problems can arise when a company holds multiple authorities. The question becomes, Who was wearing what hat and when?

Clearly, pushing the proverbial envelope when it comes to services and operations has some definite risks, and you'll want to carefully consider all your options when setting up your business.

> **Tip...**
>
> **Smart Tip**
>
> As a freight broker, you'll build your company on repeat business. If you do a good job, you'll rarely have a one-time customer. Most shippers have routine, repetitive shipments that move around the country on a predictable schedule. As you become familiar with these shipments, they become easier to handle.

How They Started

Ask a class of first-graders what they want to be when they grow up, and you'll likely hear things like doctor, firefighter, police officer and lawyer; it's highly unlikely any one of them will say "freight broker." So how did the successful freight brokers we talked with get into the business?

Bill Tucker's brokerage in Cherry Hill, New Jersey, has employed three generations of his family. His father founded the firm in 1961 by purchasing one of the few broker's licenses still operating at the time. Years later, Tucker was working in the computer industry when his father passed away unexpectedly. At first, he and his mother decided to sell the business rather than shut it down, so he helped run it while looking for a buyer. But after several months without a realistic offer, Tucker decided that he wanted the company for himself. He worked out a deal to buy the company from his mother, and now his own sons work for him. "I've never regretted it because it has been a great business," he says.

> **Stat Fact**
>
> Trucks carry 94 percent of all furniture, fixtures, and appliances for the American home.

After holding a variety of jobs in the transportation industry, Cathy Davis started MCD Transportation Inc. as a consulting and commissioned sales agency in 1986 and obtained brokerage authority in 1991. After she passed away in 2002, her daughters took over the Smyrna, Tennessee, company.

Working 9 to 5

While it's certainly possible to start a freight brokerage as a part-time business and gradually work into a full-time operation, it's not recommended. This is not a business where problems or issues can wait. You need to be accessible to your customers during regular business hours. If you're not available to answer a question or quote a rate when they need the information, they may take their business elsewhere.

There's also the image issue to consider. Whether it's a valid perception or not, many people view part-time businesses as hobbies and their operators as less than professional. Those people are not going to trust their shipments to a part-time freight broker.

If you need more income than your business will generate in its early days, consider a full-time brokerage with a part-time job on the side—but be sure the hours you work at the other job won't interfere with your brokerage; try to schedule that work for nights and weekends.

Chuck Andrews started his business in Indianapolis in 1993. Having spent his entire professional life working for trucking companies and railroads, he found the brokerage business tremendously appealing. "Out of all the transportation operations, a brokerage operation is very clean," he says. "By that, I mean it's basically a 7:30 A.M. to 5 P.M. operation. Very seldom do you have problems occur after that. Your operation runs Monday through Friday. When you're on the trucking side of it, you have all the problems. If a guy blows a tire, he's calling somebody at one or two o'clock in the morning to get money to fix it. With brokers, it's our concern—we want the freight moving on schedule—but it's not our problem because the driver is going to call his dispatcher or his company."

For 18 years, Ron Williamson worked as a corporate traffic manager and director of distribution for several major corporations. He also had experience with a railroad and a transportation consulting firm. Finally, he could no longer resist the entrepreneurial urge: He started his brokerage firm in 1981 in Bloomingdale, Illinois, and has since founded two trucking companies as well.

Specialist or Generalist?

As a broker, you have the opportunity to handle many types of freight. You may opt to simply handle general commodity freight—materials that are typically easy to handle and don't require any special attention.

Or you might want to develop some expertise in areas such as heavy equipment, oversized loads, perishable commodities or even hazardous materials.

Don't limit your specialization plan to the commonly accepted areas; instead, find your own niche. Tucker, for example, does some interesting work for retailers. One major national chain hires his company to handle the distribution of point-of-sale promotion displays that have to be delivered to hundreds of stores on the same day. It's a move that's important but not frequent enough for the retailer to maintain the required expertise in-house. Other big businesses use Tucker's company to manage shipments related to store openings and closings.

Bright Idea

If you're working with a carrier or broker now and are planning to quit to start your own brokerage, don't assume the customers you have a good relationship with will automatically follow you. It often happens, but if you're counting on that customer for early revenue, you could be in for a rude awakening.

Who's Minding the Store?

Even following deregulation, the transportation industry comes under the regulation of a number of different agencies. The least-regulated cargo is intrastate freight—shipments moving within the borders of a single state. That freight is regulated under the laws of the particular state and is also typically regulated by the state's department of transportation, department of business and professional regulation, and/or the department of revenue and taxation.

For interstate shipments—shipments moving between states—the key regulatory agency prior to 1995 was the Interstate Commerce Commission (ICC), an independent agency created by Congress in 1887 to regulate commercial activity crossing state lines. The ICC was created in response to turmoil within the railroad industry and came about after an 1886 Supreme Court ruling that said states could not regulate interstate railroads, which effectively shifted the burden of regulation to the federal government.

The commission initially possessed limited regulatory powers, but by the early 1950s its jurisdiction extended to all types of surface transportation vehicles and channels. The agency was criticized for regulatory excess and setting artificially high transportation and shipping rates. By the early 1980s, deregulation of transportation industries had stripped the ICC of most of its authority to set rates. In 1995, Congress abolished the ICC and created a Surface Transportation Board (STB) within the Department of Transportation (DOT) to perform the small number of regulatory tasks that had remained with the ICC. Today, the primary agencies that oversee motor freight transportation are the STB, the DOT, and the Federal Highway Administration.

Do You Have What It Takes?

This is not a business for the faint of heart or the shy person who is happiest shuffling papers behind a closed office door. But courage and an extroverted personality alone won't guarantee you a successful freight brokerage, either.

According to Cathy Davis, "Anyone involved in operations needs to be able to handle stress, make quick decisions, handle multiple tasks, have a good phone voice and communication skills, and possess some general business knowledge." You not only need to understand the freight industry, but you must also appreciate the business demands your customers face.

Chuck Andrews agrees that communication skills and a solid foundation in the industry are important for brokers. You need to be able to speak industry jargon to demonstrate your knowledge. "The worst thing you could do is call a shipper and start fumbling on the phone," he says. "He's never going to give you any freight because he's going to know right away that you have no knowledge of the business, and he would not trust his goods being moved with you."

Stat Fact
Trucking accounts for 78 percent of the nation's freight bill and 5 percent of the gross national product.

Ron Williamson says you've got to be "a good all-around person." That means being comfortable with the financial side, the sales side, and the operations side.

The TIA's Voltmann says, "The future for intermediaries is very bright as asset-owning carriers concentrate on what they do best, and shippers concentrate on their core competencies. Shippers and carriers need the innovation and expertise intermediaries provide. The result will be continued improvements, which will mean more choices for consumers and lower costs."

So where do you start? Chapter 2 will tell you what you need to know to lay the foundation for your freight brokerage.

2

What Does the Business Require?

The dissolution of the Interstate Commerce Commission and other aspects of transportation deregulation have left many industry players confused about what is regulated and what is not. This chapter addresses the regulatory and practical requirements of starting and running a freight brokerage.

Freight brokers must register with the Federal Highway Administration (FHWA) (contact information is listed in the Appendix). This is not a complicated process. Essentially, you must file an application (form OP-1) and pay a filing fee, obtain a $10,000 surety bond (see "Bond . . . Surety Bond") or establish a trust fund, and designate agents for service of legal process. The registration will remain valid as long as these requirements continue to be met.

The surety bond or trust fund is evidence of financial responsibility. This means you must demonstrate that you have access to that amount of liquid assets to meet your obligations and pay any potential claims. You can either use your own resources or contract with a bonding company. Evidence of a surety bond must be filed using form BMC 84; evidence of a trust fund with a financial institution must be filed using form BMC 85.

Designation of process agents means that for each state in which you have offices or in which you write contracts, you must file a designation of person on whom court process may be served.

When your application is approved, you'll receive a permit with an MC number from the FHWA that is your authority to operate as a broker within the United States.

Beyond the regulations that govern your particular operation, when you act on behalf of a person bound by law or FHWA regulations as to the transmittal of bills or payments, you must also abide by the laws or regulations that apply to that person.

In addition to federal requirements, you'll need whatever business licenses and/or operational permits that are required by your local and state governments. Check with your local planning and zoning department or city/county business license department to find out what you need and what is involved in obtaining these licences and/or permits. For example, you may need an occupational license or permit issued by your city or county, a fire department permit if you are in a commercial location and/or open to the public, and/or a sign permit.

Education and Experience

The brokers we talked with recommended working in the industry—either for a shipper, a carrier, or both—before starting your own brokerage. You'll not only gain technical expertise, but you'll also make contacts that are critical to success in this business.

Cathy Davis entered the industry as an inventory control clerk for a river terminal and then spent time working in sales for motor and air freight carriers. "I was fortunate to have been mentored by the owner of one less than truckload (LTL) carrier I worked for, and helped design a new terminal and served on an employee advisory board," she recalled. Her consulting business gave her the opportunity to learn even more about being a broker; she was an agent for brokers before becoming one

Beware!

Don't try to get around the law. Penalties for evasion of regulation by motor carriers and brokers include a civil penalty of $200 for the first violation and at least $250 for a subsequent violation.

herself, and that gave her both hands-on experience and an opportunity to build her reputation. "I highly recommend this startup method with total disclosure of intent and a legal agreement," she said. Later, she earned the Certified Transportation Broker designation through the Transportation Intermediaries Association, as did her daughters before they took over the Smyrna, Tennessee-based company.

Similarly, Chuck Andrews in Indianapolis held senior positions with a major LTL carrier, was president of a truckload (TL) carrier and has worked in railroad operations. "My whole background leading up to forming [my company] has all been in transportation," he says.

Davis believed new brokers need "a strong sales background, good business advisors, and a desire for continuing education."

Building Carrier Relationships

How can you build strong, positive relationships with carriers? "Pay on time and pay reasonable rates," said Davis. Of course, she added, having "driver-friendly" freight is a positive aspect, and communication is critical. "We use a load-matching service to help find carriers, but also network with members in various organizations. We consider the carrier a customer and extend the same degree of professionalism to a transaction with them as we do with shippers."

Establishing and building relationships with carriers may well be your biggest startup challenge. "Because of brokers who have gone out of business [owing carriers money], truckers are very careful about who they do business with," says Andrews. "If you do not have a history with that trucking company, he's not going to be very aggressive in wanting to haul your load because he doesn't know if he's going to get paid or not. Even though you have signed all the papers and you've got your surety bond, he's going to be leery until he gets that first check from you."

Tip...

Smart Tip

Know your rights: By law, common carriers are required to serve, deliver, charge reasonable rates, and not discriminate.

It's a problem that only time can solve. "It took us quite a few years to build up our business," Andrews says. "We currently have close to 7,000 truckers under contract to move our freight." When he adds a new trucker, he presents himself as a reliable, professional broker by sending an information package that includes

▲

Bond . . . Surety Bond

Many people do not have a clear understanding of what a bond actually does. Basically, it is an amount of money that you post to guarantee that you will do something you've promised to do. Probably the most common way you hear the term "bond" used is in criminal cases. When someone is arrested and charged with a crime, he or she can put up an amount of money (or something else of value) to guarantee an appearance in court. If the person shows up as promised, the money is returned; if he or she is a no show, the money is forfeited.

Because many people do not have the cash on hand to post the full amount of a required bond, they turn to a bonding company. The bonding company charges a percentage of the total bond to put up whatever amount of money is required. The money the bonding company collects is a fee and is not refundable. In addition to charging the fee, the bonding company may also ask you to post collateral, such as real estate or equipment.

Here's where the confusion on bonds often occurs: A bond is not insurance you purchase; it is the collateral for a promise. And if you use a bonding company, you are still ultimately responsible for the total amount of the bond, not just the fee you paid to the company.

In the case of a freight broker, the surety bond guarantees that you will meet all your contractual obligations to your customers and that you can pay any claims immediately. If you use a bonding company and that company pays any claims on your behalf, you must repay the company, usually within 80 to 90 days. If you fail to repay and have posted collateral, you will likely lose that collateral.

information on the company, a listing of key personnel, bank information, and carrier references. "The hard part is getting that first load moved and then being able to build on that for your credit references."

It's important to understand the economics of the trucking business when you negotiate payment terms with your carriers. In the past, ICC regulations dictated that freight bills be paid within seven days; today, since deregulation, that is negotiable. But carriers operate on very narrow margins and pay most of their expenses on a given load before they ever pick up the load, so cash flow is as critical to them as it is to the broker.

Some brokers would prefer not to have to pay the carrier until they get paid themselves, and while that would be a safe approach for the broker, you won't find carriers very enthusiastic about it. "Carriers take the stand that the reason they are

Beware!
Be sure to fully check the references and credentials of all the carriers you use before you ever give them the first load. If you fail to do so and a problem occurs, you could find yourself responsible for the damages.

using a broker is so they don't have to do credit checks on the customers or do the sales and service that we provide," says Cherry Hill, New Jersey, freight broker Bill Tucker. "It's one of the reasons the carriers will sell to you a little lower than they would bill the shipper direct. The carriers are saying, 'You handle the credit for your customer base and you pay me whether you get paid or not.' It just keeps it simpler and cleaner."

Tucker notes that there may be times, such as with high-volume shippers or a special seasonal situation, when the billing can escalate rapidly, and the broker and carrier agree to share the financial risk. But those types of contract clauses are the exceptions. Says Tucker, "I would say that in 99 percent of the transactions, the broker does the collections and pays the trucker every penny owed."

Banking On Your Banker

Solid banking relationships are critical for brokers. Andrews says it's not unusual for a new broker to need a line of credit in the range of $250,000 to $300,000 to be able to pay carriers before being paid by the shippers. "If you don't pay the trucks in a timely fashion, they won't haul your freight. If you have nobody to haul your freight, you have no business," he says. "Other than getting your licensing and insurance, setting up with a good banker is probably at the top of the list."

Of course, you don't want to walk empty-handed into a bank you've never done business with and ask for a major line of credit. "You have to know your banker really well. Go in with a business plan. It also helps if you have been doing business with that bank and they know you," Andrews says. "You have to have an excellent credit record, because [as a broker] you have no assets for them to come after."

Put together a package that clearly demonstrates to the bank that you are not a credit risk and that they'll benefit by establishing a line of credit for you.

In these days of banking mergers and acquisitions, along with personnel turnover, it's a good idea to have relationships with more than one bank. If you have a single line of credit with one bank and that bank gets sold, you could find your line of credit canceled through no fault of your own. Or if you have a strong relationship with a loan officer who gets promoted, transferred, or changes jobs, you may find the new loan officer not as receptive to your needs. Protect yourself by making sure you always have a financial backup to turn to.

Start Me Up

The following table will give you an idea of the necessary start-up expenses for a freight brokerage. Where your operation falls within the ranges depends on whether you start as a homebased business or in a commercial location, and whether you hire employees right away or do everything yourself in the beginning. The suggested operating capital should be enough to cover the first three months of operation and must be sufficient to cover paying carriers before you are paid by shippers.

Rent	$0–$1,000
Equipment	$6,000–$22,000
Licenses/tax deposits	$200–$400
Advertising/marketing	$500–$1,500
Utilities/phone	$100–$300
Professional services	$200–$750
Payroll	$0–$5,000
Supplies	$300–$500
Insurance (first quarter)	$700–$1,400
Suggested operating capital	$5,000–$250,000 (cash or line of credit)

Those Critical Customers

Certainly you need strong relationships with your carriers and bankers, but the most essential outside element of your business is your customer base. Though you'll do a certain amount of cold-calling as you market your business, most of your customers will come through referrals, contacts, and networking. You can use your network to get in the door, but remember, this is about business, not just about friendship. "Just because you know someone doesn't mean they are going to give you the business if your pricing isn't competitive," says Andrews.

Of course, there's more involved than just pricing. Communication is essential. Let customers know what's happening with their shipments; Andrews says this means almost-daily contact. Shippers need the comfort of knowing when their freight is moving as scheduled and the opportunity to react appropriately if it isn't. Most shippers can deal with mechanical, weather, or traffic delays as long as they know about them. Don't let them find out from their customers that shipments weren't delivered as scheduled; let them know ahead of time that, for whatever reason, the truck isn't going to make it, and when they can expect delivery.

Record-Keeping Requirements

The Code of Federal Regulations is very specific about what types of records you must maintain. While you may keep a master list of shippers and carriers to avoid repeating the information, you are required to keep a record of each transaction. That record must show:

- the name and address of the consignor (shipper)
- the name, address and registration number of the originating motor carrier
- the bill of lading (see the Glossary) or freight bill number
- the amount of compensation received by the broker for the brokerage service performed and the name of the payer
- a description of any nonbrokerage service performed in connection with each shipment or other activity, the amount of compensation received for the service, and the name of the payer
- the amount of any freight charges collected by the broker and the date of payment to the carrier

Beware!
Even though your contract will prohibit it, you may occasionally work with a carrier that will approach your client directly. This is bad business, and it's likely that a carrier operating with such a lack of integrity won't be in business long. Nonetheless, be aware that it can happen, and if you find out about it, be prepared to take the appropriate legal steps, including cease and desist orders and suing for lost revenue.

Be Careful What You Say

There may be situations when you're with other brokers—or even shippers and carriers—and the conversation centers around customers you have in common. Protect the privacy of your customers and the confidentiality of their businesses. Not only is this a sound professional business practice, but you are prohibited by law from disclosing information to an unrelated party that may be used to the detriment of the shipper or consignee.

You must keep these records for a period of three years, and each party to a particular transaction has a right to review the records relating to that transaction.

Golden Rules for Transportation Intermediaries

1. Know the company you are dealing with. Establish criteria that must be met by the parties with whom you will have a business transaction. Create a checklist and use it every time you establish a new relationship.

2. Create a procedure for tracking the performance of the companies with which you establish a relationship. Review performance often.

3. Take action early if things begin to go wrong. Line staff must communicate recurring problems to management.

4. Make sure there are no surprises! Be willing to convey why you need information so people can be supportive and participatory.

5. Provide load confirmation in a timely manner—15 to 30 minutes. Minimum information: consignor/consignee; origin/destination; commodity; value; rate; pickup and delivery schedule; pallet considerations; and any special requirements. Immediately return Rate Agreement.

6. Immediately convey "change" information. Time is of the essence. People can generally accommodate changes if given enough notice.

7. Be a role model in developing cooperative service attitudes. Provide proper training so employees can be effective problem-solvers.

8. Provide accurate invoices promptly. Provide Proof of Deliveries as requested.

9. Carriers and intermediaries should provide 24-hour access to each other.

10. Appreciate the skills, experience, and professionalism brought to each transaction by all involved parties. Express this appreciation sincerely and frequently.

11. Be straightforward in all contractual and financial matters.

These principles were established during the Joint Trust Forum between Transportation Brokers Conference of America and National Association of Small Trucking Companies in Nashville, Tennessee, in 1994.

Operations

The basic concept of freight brokering is pretty simple: A shipper (or consignor, as they're sometimes referred to) calls you with a load. You complete your own internal paperwork and check with your carriers to see who has a vehicle available. If you already have a relationship with a carrier, you fax it an addendum to your basic contract that describes this particular load and the rate. If the carrier agrees, the company's representative signs the document and faxes it back. (If you don't already have a relationship with the carrier, you'll need to set up a carrier/broker agreement before you finalize the deal on the first shipment.) Next, the carrier dispatches the driver. It's a good idea to require that the driver call you to confirm that the load has been picked up and again when it has been delivered.

After the shipment has been delivered, the carrier will send you an invoice and the original bill of lading. You invoice your customer (the shipper), pay the trucker, and then, ideally, do the whole thing again with another shipment.

Facts on File

When you arrange a shipment, you'll need information from both the shipper and the carrier. Much of this information should be kept on file in your office.

Shipper Information

Maintaining information on shippers helps you provide better customer service and saves you from having to take the time to ask the same questions with each shipment. Keep the following information:

- Company name
- Physical address
- Billing address, if different from physical address
- All telephone numbers (cell phones, voice, fax, pagers), including any toll-free numbers
- Contact people (including traffic and shipping managers, freight payable person, and anyone else you may deal with)
- Type of freight shipped (machinery, produce, chemicals, etc.)
- Type of equipment (trucks) required
- Pallet exchange requirements
- Other special requirements
- Any other pickup information you require (such as warehouse locations or other distribution points)

This information will not change frequently, but you should always make sure you have current information. Immediately update anything you find out about during the course of handling a shipment, such as a change in personnel or a new phone number. Once a year, you should call each customer and review the information. Pitch this exercise as a benefit; tell the customer that you have a policy of checking your files periodically to confirm their completeness and accuracy, and you want to go over what you have on file to confirm that it is correct. When you are finished, ask if there's anything else you should know that would help you serve the customer better, or if there are any shipping needs you don't know about that you could help with.

Of course, with each shipment you'll need to know the destination company's name, address, contact person and phone number. If your customers ship to the same places over and over, you'll want to keep this information on file to make it easier and faster to prepare the documentation for each load.

This information is not only necessary for your carriers (how else will they know where to take the freight if you don't tell them?), but it also gives you another potential shipper. If the consignee (the recipient of the shipment) is a manufacturer, they may have goods your carrier can pick up after dropping off your initial shipper's load. If the consignee has freight to send back to the initial shipper—or even someone else in the same area—and your carrier can handle this load as well, the carrier gets a very productive round trip. The trucker does not have to return empty (which means generating no revenue) or take the time and effort to find a load on its own.

Be sure to find out in advance if the shipper requires a pallet exchange, which saves carriers from having to return pallets to shippers and saves shippers from having to replace pallets all the time. It works like this: Many types of goods are loaded onto pallets, which are then loaded onto trucks. Many drivers carry empty pallets in their trucks. When they receive a load on pallets, they exchange their empty pallets for those used by the shipper for the materials just picked up. When the driver reaches the destination, the loaded pallets are swapped for empty ones, replenishing the driver's supply.

When you complete a load sheet for each shipment, include the identification numbers of the tractor and trailer that hauled the load. The carriers will provide you with their equipment numbers; it's standard procedure.

Carrier Information

Keep up-to-date information on carriers even if you don't have any loads for them at the moment. By maintaining files on carriers, you will know immediately which routes they travel and what kinds of trucks they have. This will help you select a carrier quickly when a shipper calls. Keep the following information:

- Carrier's name

- Type of carrier (contract, common, etc.)
- Physical address
- Billing address, if different from physical address
- All telephone numbers (cell phones, voice, fax, pagers), including any toll-free numbers
- Contact person (in most cases, the dispatcher)
- Other terminals, phone numbers, and contacts
- Type and size of equipment available
- Motor carrier's license number
- Federal tax identification number
- Whether or not the carrier offers pallet exchanges
- Carrier's traffic lanes and backhaul requirements

Beyond the basic information about a carrier that helps you make the selection, you should obtain the following additional data before you actually give that carrier a load:

- Copy of current insurance certificates and updates
- Certificate of authority
- Copy of current general commodity tariff and updates (if applicable)

These key documents prove that the carrier is licensed to transport freight and is insured if cargo is lost or damaged. You should not only confirm that the carrier is insured, but also note when the insurance expires. When that date arrives, check with the carrier for proof that the coverage has been renewed. Certificates of insurance usually include a provision that the holder will be notified by the company upon cancellation of coverage.

In addition to these items, ask your carriers for a statement that they assume full responsibility for paying all fuel taxes, including ton mile taxes (taxes based on the weight and distance), in all states through which they travel. Also, while on lease or contract, they should pay fines for any and all violations incurred. Though carriers generally make it a standard part of their business operation to pay these fines, you should obtain a written agreement to that effect and place it in your files.

You should also retain any correspondence, agreements, rate quotations, policy changes, memos, etc., along with copies of all contracts, bills of lading, and invoices you send or receive.

Finding Carriers

There are tens of thousands of carriers operating in the United States. Your job as a broker is to identify the ones that provide services your customers need and to confirm their reliability before using them.

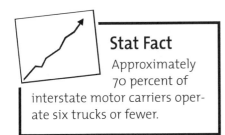

Stat Fact
Approximately 70 percent of interstate motor carriers operate six trucks or fewer.

You'll find carriers listed in a number of directories and trade magazines. Word-of-mouth is also a good way to find carriers; as you're out there networking, pay attention to what others are saying about particular trucking companies, and follow up on good reports.

You can also look for trucks at truck stops and on the road. When you see trucks that are clean and well-maintained, speak to the driver and find out something about the company. If it isn't practical to speak to the driver, make a note of the company name and headquarters location (it will be on the truck or the cab), and give the company a call.

"For 18 years, I've written down the names of trucking companies I see on the highway," says Bloomingdale, Illinois, freight broker Ron Williamson. "I'll call that company and ask if it has any extra trucks it can provide us."

Of course, don't overlook the internet as a source for carriers. There are a number of online databases that allow shippers and carriers to post their freight and equipment needs. (See the Appendix for a sample listing of these databases.)

Once you've found a carrier that might be useful, you need more information before you turn a load over to it. Ask for copies of the carrier's certificate of authority, current insurance certificates, and current tariff. You should also get references from satisfied customers and take the time to check those references. Finally, check a credit reporting bureau or financial rating service to find out what the carrier's financial condition is. You want to be sure the carriers you work with are reliable and financially sound.

Avoid using major carriers that have terminals all over the country. These carriers do not take loads directly from pickup to destination; rather, they relay a load from one terminal point to another. This process takes additional time and increases the amount of handling, which increases the risk of loss or damage. It's better if the driver who picks up the load delivers it.

Some carriers use a procedure called pooling, where loads are dropped and left until a driver with the proper equipment and destination is available to pick them up. Though this may sound like an effective practice, it causes delays in transit time, and you should avoid carriers that employ this method. Such a policy will give you a competitive edge by enabling your shippers to meet tight delivery schedules.

Stat Fact
It costs carriers an average of $550 per day to let a truck sit, waiting to find a load to avoid an empty backhaul. "That's why brokers are so much in demand," says Bloomingdale, Illinois, freight broker Ron Williamson. "If it's Tuesday, you don't want that driver sitting in town until Wednesday."

Rates and Commissions

In the beginning, it's a good idea to handle FTLs only because they're easier to deal with than less-than-truckload (LTL) shipments. It's impractical for many carriers to handle a partial load; you would need to arrange for the driver to pick up two or more LTL shipments headed for the same destination. That may seem a bit over-whelming when you're just getting started, but as you gain experience, you'll be able to handle both FTL and LTL shipments easily.

Freight charges are based on a number of variables, but the two main factors are the weight of the load and the distance it must travel. Rates are also affected by the type of truck needed, whether the driver needs to make one or more stops to pick up the freight, and whether the driver needs to make more than one stop to deliver the goods. Each shipment is entitled to one pickup and one delivery with no extra charge; you can usually negotiate the rate for additional stops with the carrier.

Before you begin shopping for rates for specific shipments, get an idea of the current "going rates" for the types of shipments you're likely to be handling. You can do this by requesting copies of tariffs from several carriers and studying them.

Many shippers—especially large companies with experienced traffic departments—will not leave it up to you to quote a rate, but will tell you how much they are willing to pay. If this amount is unreasonable, you'll need to negotiate with the shipper or decline to handle the load.

Calculating freight pricing is not a simple process. Carriers negotiate rates based on commodity, value, equipment availability, volume, customer service factors, and payment history, among other things. As a broker, you need to know what the market issues are, as well as what can cause increases or decreases in the per-mile rate, such as driver shortages, fuel surcharges, seasonal changes, toll roads, and so on.

Your income is generated by the commissions you earn on each load. You'll be paid one of two ways: You can bill the shipper the amount you are going to pay the carrier plus the amount of your commission, or the carrier can bill the shipper directly and then pay you a commission from its revenue.

Stat Fact

Annual revenue from trucking each year is around $362 billion—more than ten times the revenue generated in the railroad industry.

The most common way to handle billing and commissions is to have the carrier bill you and then you bill your customers. Cherry Hill, New Jersey, freight broker Bill Tucker says this is much easier and less confusing for your customers than if they are billed directly by the carrier. If the carrier bills your customer directly, your customers will receive

Know Your Limits

As a broker, by law you may not charge or receive compensation from a motor carrier for brokerage service where you own or have a material interest in the shipment. You are also not able to exercise control over the shipment because you own the shipper, the shipper owns your company, or there is a common ownership of the two.

In addition, you may not give or offer to give anything of value to any shipper or consignee (or their officers or employees) other than inexpensive advertising items distributed for promotional purposes.

---

multiple styles of bills on a variety of billing cycles, and they will have to do the extra work of matching up the bill to the shipment. "When their computer generates a bill of lading for the broker and the carrier bills them, it gets confusing," Tucker says. "Nowadays, almost all freight brokers bill the shipper and pay the carrier. It's much simpler for the shipper."

Your commission is negotiable and you can get whatever the traffic will bear. The average broker's commission is between 5 and 11 percent of the shipping charges, sometimes higher, and a new broker can typically expect to earn between 8 and 10 percent.

"It all comes down to negotiating," says Indianapolis freight broker Chuck Andrews. "If you're in a highly competitive market area—like in Atlanta, where there is a lot of freight and not very many trucks—your [commission will be much lower than the industry average]."

Keep in mind that your commission is your gross revenue, and out of that you must pay your overhead: rent, taxes, payroll, sales commissions, utilities, debts, etc. Ron Williamson estimates that most brokers are lucky to earn a net profit of 1 to 2 percent after expenses.

Although you, your carriers, and your shippers need to agree on the total freight expenses for shipments, the prices of transporting freight can be broken down into smaller units. Those numbers are used to help carriers measure their own profitability and by shippers to set prices of their goods and determine profit levels. For example, carriers are interested in the total fee for any given trip, and they also want to know their fee per mile. Shippers are often interested in the cost by weight, typically measured in 100-pound units, and referred to as cost per hundred weight (abbreviated "cwt"). These numbers are easy to calculate with simple arithmetic.

Profit Prophet

When someone is considering starting a business, often one of his or her first questions is, "How soon will I start making money?" What they really mean is, "How soon will I start making a profit?" For a freight brokerage, the answer to that question is "It depends."

You'll start generating revenue with your first shipment. How long you take to actually begin making a profit will depend on the size of your operation, your monthly overhead expenses, how many customers you had when you opened your doors, and the thoroughness and aggressiveness of your business plan. Indianapolis freight broker Chuck Andrews says that if you have shippers lined up from the beginning and you're aggressive, you could be profitable in 90 days. But if you only have a few customers and aren't moving a lot of freight, it could take a year or more.

Quoting Rates

To quote a rate for a customer, follow these ten steps:

1. Find out the point of origin.

2. Find out the destination.

3. Determine the gross weight of the load.

4. Ask if the carrier will need to make stop-offs or split pickups.

5. Check whether pallets are required.

6. Find out when the load(s) will be ready for pickup.

7. Find out when the load(s) can be/need to be delivered.

8. Ask if appointments are necessary at origin or destination.

9. Find out who gets billed for the freight charges.

10. Obtain the frequency and number of similar shipments.

With this information, you'll be able to contact carriers for quotes that will be accurate. Few things are more frustrating in this business than to quote a rate based on incomplete information and to later find out the customer needs extra services you have to charge for, which means you have to tell them the final bill will be higher than your original estimate. (Needless to say, customers don't like this.)

Documents

Once you match a load with a carrier, you must fill out a number of forms. First, you and the carrier need to enter into an agreement covering current and future dealings. The Transportation Intermediaries Association provides sample agreements in its New Broker Kit (see Appendix under "Publications and Training Resources" for contact information), but the freight brokers we talked with recommended that you develop your own contracts, agreements, and forms, customizing them to your particular operation.

Once you have a carrier agreement on file, you need to send the carrier a load confirmation and rate agreement form for each specific load. When the carrier picks up the load from the shipper, the shipper will give the carrier a bill of lading listing the goods being transported and any special arrangements the driver needs to make for the load. When the driver reaches the consignee (recipient of the shipment), he needs to have someone there sign for the load. If an independent contractor unloads the freight at the consignee's location, the driver needs to obtain a contract labor receipt from this worker.

Depending on your arrangement with the carrier, the driver or trucking company will invoice you, the shipper, or the consignee for transportation services.

Carrier/Broker Agreement

The carrier/broker agreement outlines the terms under which you will work with a given carrier. It's designed to apply to all the dealings you have with a particular carrier and should also provide for any future changes.

When writing the carrier/broker agreement, make sure to do all the following:

- Note the carrier's motor carrier (MC) or license number, full corporate name, and address.

- If you will be working with this carrier on a contract basis, state that the freight and rates will be negotiated for each shipment.

- State that the carrier is liable for any damage or loss to the freight that occurs while the carrier transports it.

- Note that the carrier is responsible for any personal injury or damage to vehicles or equipment that occurs while the freight is in the carrier's possession.

Tip...

Smart Tip

In most cases, when a broker and a carrier are entering into a new relationship, it is the broker who creates and introduces the contract. Though the carrier may negotiate certain points, it is typically the responsibility of the broker to handle this administrative task.

- State when the carrier will receive payment and what the carrier must provide before you will pay (such as bills of lading).

(For a sample Carrier/Broker Agreement, turn to page 27.)

Load Confirmation and Rate Agreement

Once a carrier agrees to move a given load, you should complete and send a load confirmation and rate agreement form. This should include the name and address of both the shipper and the consignee, a trip number (for tracking purposes), any information on extra pickups or stops, pickup and delivery dates, a brief description of the commodity to be shipped, and your commission or brokerage fee structure. (For a sample Load Confirmation and Rate Agreement, see page 28.)

Bill of Lading

At the time of the pickup, the shipper will provide the driver with a bill of lading. This form will include information on the nature and size of the load, its destination, and any required special handling. The driver signs the bill of lading as an acknowledgment of receiving the load described by the shipper.

The bill of lading is prepared and handled by the shipper and the carrier. As the broker, you will not be directly concerned with it, but you need to keep a signed copy in your files. The carrier usually sends this to you, along with its invoice for transportation services.

Contract Labor Receipt

Drivers may occasionally work with contract laborers who unload trucks once they reach the consignee. If they do, the laborer will give the driver a contract labor receipt, which the carrier sends to you. The driver or carrier pays the laborer and turns to you for reimbursement. If your shipper is willing to cover this cost, pay it. Even if your shipper doesn't want to pay for contract labor, you may want to consider absorbing the expense so you can maintain good relations with the driver and carrier.

(See page 29 for a sample Contract Labor Receipt.)

Stat Fact

According to the American Trucking Association, motor carriers collect 87 percent of total revenue earned by all modes of transportation.

Invoices

After making the delivery and obtaining proof of delivery, the carrier sends you an invoice, along with the bill of lading. With these documents, you can prepare your own invoice to send to the shipper. (Unless, of course, the carrier bills the shipper directly.)

Carrier/Broker Agreement

This agreement is entered into between Jiffy Freight Brokers, hereinafter referred to as "Broker," and _____, hereinafter referred to as "Carrier."

Whereas Broker is a transportation broker engaged in the business of selling or negotiating transportation with ICC Authority MC#128673, and whereas Carrier is a motor carrier operating in interstate commerce, with contact authority MC#_____.

1. The terms of the agreement shall be continuous from signing date.
2. Freight and rate shall be set and agreed upon at the time of each movement.
3. Termination of this agreement can be instituted by either party by giving thirty (30) days' notice in writing to the other party.
4. The Carrier shall be liable for all loss, damage, or liability incurred by transportation of property arranged for by the Broker while being transported by the Carrier.
5. In the event of disagreement or dispute, and if legal action is taken, the prevailing party will be entitled to legal fees.
6. Carrier will be paid within 15 days of receipt of clean bills.
7. This agreement contains the entire contract agreement and no additions can be made unless in writing or initialing by both parties.

In witness whereof, the parties hereto have signed their names on this _____ day of _____, 20_____,
in _____.
     City   State

Company: Jiffy Freight Brokers   Company: _____

           333 ABC Ln.   _____

           Peoria, IL 92688   _____

By: _____   By: _____

Witness: _____   Witness: _____

Load Confirmation and Rate Agreement

 Jiffy Freight Brokers

Fax date: 11/12/05	Trip number: 5546
Carrier: Watson Trucking	Carrier fax: (000) 555-5555

Driver must call JFB for dispatch. The following is for information only.

Shipper:
    Bob's Frozen Dinners
    Kansas City, MO
    Extra Pickups:

Consignee:
    Adler Refrigeration
    Columbus, OH
    Extra Stops:

Pickup date: 11/10/05
I.O.# 4418
Comments:

Deliver date: 11/12/05
Commodity: Corn Dog

_____

_____

_____

Jiffy Freight Brokers charges 9% brokerage without advance and 11% with advance. If you need more than 50% of truck pay in advances, brokerage will be 15%. JFB will not advance more than 65% of truck pay.

Gross Agreed Charges: $500.00

Please refer to the TRIP NUMBER on your invoice: TRIP# 5546
All invoices must include a signed delivery receipt and be sent to:

    Jiffy Freight Brokers
    1111 Baker St.
    Columbus, OH 11111

The undersigned hereby acknowledges as correct and accepts the referenced shipment on behalf of carrier. It is agreed that the charges indicated above are inclusive. Invoicing by the carrier and payment by Jiffy Freight Brokers creates a valid contract of carrier shipment.

Please sign this confirmation and fax to JFB at (000) 555-5556.

_____   _____

Watson Trucking   Jiffy Freight Brokers

Contract Labor Receipt

Being the recipient of the below listed contract price, and an independent businessperson and contractor, I am fully responsible for the payment of my own taxes thereon, including self-employment taxes, income taxes, and all other applicable taxes.

I contract to load _____ unload _____

loads of _____ for the amount of

$_____.

Signed (Contractor) _____

Social Security or Fed I.D. # _____

Street address _____

City _____ State _____ Zip code _____

Driver _____

Date _____

Your invoice should include the billing date, the dates of pickup and delivery, the origin, and destination, what was shipped (commodity, pieces and total weight), and additional fees (such as fees for exceeding weight limits or charges for contract labor). Bill your shipper as soon as you receive the complete invoice and bill of lading from your carrier.

If the shipper is sending the delivery "collect," then you bill the consignee rather than the shipper. The shipper should provide you with billing information on these shipments. (See page 30 for a sample Invoice.)

Stat Fact

Commercial trucks pay more than $30.5 billion yearly in federal and state highway user taxes, which fund road improvement and maintenance.

Invoice

Jiffy Freight Brokers

1111 Baker Street
Columbus, OH 11111

Invoice: 005546   Date: 11/12/05

Bill to:

P/U: 11/10/05   Del: 11/12/05

Bob's Frozen Dinners   Carr: WATTRU   Trip# 005546
2222 E. Havisham Rd.
Kansas City, MO 00000   P/O: 4481   B/L:

Shipper: Bob's Frozen Dinners   Consignee: Adler Refrigeration
BOBFRO   2222 E. Havisham Rd.   ADREF   3333 Cratchett Ln.
           Kansas City, MO 00000   Columbus, OH 00000

Pieces	Description	Identifier	Weight	Rate	Charges
	Corn Dogs		PE		$700.00
	Unloading				45.00
	Invoice Total				$745.00

This account is due and payable in 7 days.

Contract of Carriage

A contract of carriage is not a document itself, but it's important that you understand the concept and what it includes. Many otherwise well-informed transportation professionals view the bill of lading as a contract of carriage—a common misconception. "A bill of lading is certainly a receipt used in a contract of carriage, but there are many elements required by that contract that are generally not stated on the bill of lading," says Bill Tucker. "Some examples: the price agreed to in the contract, all the services to be provided, rules to be used to handle exceptions, and accessorial charges that may be applicable."

What makes up a contract of carriage? "A contract of carriage between a common carrier and a shipper (with or without a broker being involved) usually consists of some form of bill of lading, whether 'standard' or not, plus all the tariff provisions, pricing, rules, and service descriptions," Tucker says. "Also part of the total contract is the intent of the parties; the regulatory rules that must be followed, whether federal, state or local; and all the other 'usage of trade' and precedent within which this transaction has occurred."

Are You on a Mission?

At any given moment, most business owners have a very clear understanding of the mission of their companies. They know what they are doing, how and where it's being done, and who their customers are. Problems can arise, however, when that mission is not clearly articulated into a statement, written down and communicated to others.

Even in a very small company, a written mission statement helps everyone involved see the big picture and keeps them focused on the true goals of the business. At a minimum, your mission statement should define who your primary customers are, identify the services you provide, and describe the geographical location in which you operate. A mission statement should be short—usually just one sentence and certainly no more than three. A good idea is to cap it at 100 words. Anything longer than that isn't a mission statement and will probably confuse your employees. Your mission statement doesn't have to be clever or catchy—just accurate.

To develop an effective mission statement, ask yourself these questions:

- Why does my company exist? Whom do we serve? What is our purpose?
- What are our strengths, weaknesses, opportunities, and threats?
- Considering the above, along with our expertise and resources, what business should we be in?
- What is important to us? What do we stand for?

Smyrna, Tennessee-based MCD Transportation's mission statement reads: "To provide our customers with dependable transportation services based on fair and competitive pricing programs with an emphasis on customer service for all concerned parties. To be receptive to customers' needs and react in a professional and timely manner. To recognize customers, carriers and vendors as our only assets for continued success." Not only is the mission statement used as a marketing tool, but employees are encouraged to periodically review it and suggest any changes they think are needed.

(Use the Mission Statement Worksheet on page 33 to help you write one for your business.)

Seasonal Issues

It's likely that no industry is more affected by seasonal issues than transportation. The volume and type of freight moving often depends on the time of year. At times, there will be an abundance of trucks and drivers eager to haul loads, and other times balancing the federal budget will look like a simpler task than finding a single truck and driver. For example, even though you may not handle produce, produce season can cause a lack of trucks that affects your ability to serve your customers. Another busy season is, of course, the fourth quarter, as holiday merchandise and year-end orders are moving.

In addition to equipment availability, there's also the issue of weather. Snow and ice can create dangerous driving conditions and affect transit times. Fog and rain can be year-round problems in various parts of the country. In dry seasons, areas prone to wild-fires may experience road closures due to heavy smoke and fire jumping across highways. Tornadoes usually last just a few minutes and hurricanes take less than a day to pass through an area, but the damage they leave behind can have a major impact on the ability of truckers to move cargo.

Beyond the mechanics of seasonal issues—getting the freight on trucks and moved—is the impact of seasons on your revenue. If possible, build your customer base with accounts that are not strongly seasonal in nature. Expect some slowdowns at certain times of the year; prepare for those periods and use the time to evaluate your business and deal with any internal issues that need attention. You can also increase your sales efforts during slow periods. It's very important to understand your customer base so you can accurately predict and prepare for the slow periods, especially when it comes to adjusting for a drop in cash flow.

The Impact of 9/11 on Brokers

The terrorist attacks of 9/11 have prompted increased security measures for all modes of transportation. An issue of particular impact on brokers has to do with who is driving the trucks. "You used to be able to drive right up to the shipping dock, get your load and go," says Joe Workman, president of Transportation Resources Inc., a freight management company with headquarters in Winter Park, Florida. "Now, in

Mission Statement Worksheet

To develop an effective mission statement, ask yourself these four questions:

1. Why does my company exist? Who do we serve? What is our purpose?

_____

_____

_____

2. What are our strengths, weaknesses, opportunities, and threats?

_____

_____

_____

3. Considering the above, along with our expertise and resources, what business should we be in?_____

_____

_____

_____

4. What is important to us? What do we stand for? _____

_____

_____

_____

Now that you've answered those questions, you are ready to write your own mission statement. Use the area below.

_____

_____

_____

_____

many cases, drivers have to show identification before they are admitted to the premises, and some companies require drivers to be pre-qualified before picking up a load. Shippers are more concerned than they've ever been about who is hauling their freight."

Workman says many shippers want to be able to maintain communication with drivers by either cell phone or satellite. "If drivers don't have reliable on-the-road communication means, we can't use them, and that cuts back on our available trucks."

If you want to handle air freight, you should know that airlines now require cargo to come from known shippers. "Somebody with the carrier has to know you and vouch for you," says Workman. "It's harder now for new people to do business."

Customers who ship sensitive or hazardous materials have special requirements, and you should find out what those are as far in advance as possible. Workman advises, "Know your customers—know who they are, what they do, and what you're picking up."

What Can Go Wrong?

In the freight business, the ability to deal with problems is essential. What can go wrong? Everything! And no matter how well you handle your part of the process, there are certain things that are out of your control but for which your shippers will look to you for assistance and solutions.

Because brokers are not carriers, they are generally not liable for loss or damage of a shipment while being transported. They can, however, be held liable if they are negligent, or if they offer services other than brokerage. Aside from the liability issue, part of your service package should include assisting your customers with problems whether you are responsible or not.

Transit Delays

It's virtually impossible to list all the reasons freight might be delayed in transit. Weather is always a major concern. Trucks break down, traffic gets heavy, highways are closed, drivers get sick—and your customers will expect you to deal with it all. Cathy Davis of MCD Transportation in Smyrna, Tennessee, recalled a nightmare of a situation involving the proverbial "driver from hell." She said, "The freight was held hostage [for payment] by an owner/operator even though the company had signed a contract agreeing to the terms. We had to pay air freight charges to ship more material to keep the customer's production line going."

Most of your problems won't be that dramatic, but any time the freight does not move precisely as expected, your customers will be looking to you for situation management and information.

Cargo Loss or Damage Claims

As the broker, you are not responsible for cargo loss or damage claims. Keep in mind that although common carriers are generally liable for loss or damage to the goods they carry, they are not responsible for losses occurring due to acts of God, war, or government; through defaults on the part of the shipper; or for losses resulting from the nature of the goods. Whatever the reason for the loss or damage, you need to understand the process of dealing with claims and be prepared to assist your shippers when necessary.

If the driver does not review the bill of lading and inspect the freight before the shipment is loaded, the carrier doesn't really have any options other than to pay a claim if the cargo is damaged or short when it arrives at the destination. There will be times when the loading crew makes mistakes but realizes them after the fact and initiates a bill of lading change, which relieves the driver and carrier of potential claim responsibility. But you cannot rely on them to

> **Beware!**
> Sometimes employees of the shipper or consignee, or at the warehouses those companies use, try to cover damages and shortages they cause by trying to make it look like the carrier's fault. Protect yourself and your carriers while maintaining your relationship with customers and warehouses by insisting that drivers do their jobs thoroughly, which means checking the load and making complete documentation.

do so, and drivers should examine each load to be sure the documents match the shipment, and sign for exactly what is received.

There will be times when it's impractical or impossible for the driver to thoroughly inspect a shipment. For example, if the carrier drops a trailer at the shipper's location to be loaded by the shipper's employees and then picked up later for transport, the driver won't know what went on the trailer. Or if the shipper assembles and shrink-wraps pallets of boxes, the driver may not be able to precisely count the number of boxes on each pallet. In those cases, the driver should write "shipper's load and count" and/or "contents and condition unknown" on the bill of lading, which shifts the responsibility for shortages, overages and concealed damage back to the shipper.

Tip...

Smart Tip

If a particular driver or carrier repeatedly incurs damage claims, especially if they are filed by different shippers, find out why. The drivers may be doing a sloppy job of securing the freight or they may be stealing some of the goods they haul. You need to identify and correct the problem at its source or stop using that driver or carrier.

At the destination, the consignee's receiving person should also inspect and count the shipment and note any discrepancies or visible damage on the delivery receipt.

When you learn of a potential claim—possibly from the shipper, consignee, or driver—immediately notify the carrier and dispatcher. Sometimes they hear of a possible problem from the driver making the delivery and let you know. Or you might not find out about a claim until you receive the proof of delivery and bill of lading with damage notations.

Not every damage notation results in a claim. For example, it's possible for the contents to be fine even though the exterior of a box was damaged.

How the claim is handled often depends on the amount in question and the history and reputation of the shipper. For a small claim where damage was clearly noted on the delivery receipt, the carrier will probably pay without a detailed investigation. For a larger claim, the carrier may send out an inspector to take a look at the damaged goods. A carrier can decline to pay a claim if it determines that the cause of the damage was inadequate packaging, so consignees should keep the damaged items and the packing materials until the claim is resolved.

Shippers usually have standard forms used to file their claims. All you need to do is provide the shipper with the name and address of the carrier in question and, if necessary, assist them in reaching a fair and prompt settlement.

If your shipper is not familiar with procedures for filing a claim, explain that he or she will need to submit the following information to the carrier on a signed form:

- Carrier's name and address

- Total claim amount
- Date of pickup
- Date of delivery
- Claim history
- Shipper's full name and address
- Consignee's full name and address
- Damages or shortages

The shipper will also need to attach any required or appropriate supporting documentation, including:

- Freight bill
- Bill of lading
- Invoice
- Inspection report, if any
- Itemized statement of loss

The carrier has 30 days to either pay the claim or acknowledge the claim and advise the shipper what else it needs to process the claim. Federal law requires carriers to investigate claims promptly and either settle the claim within 120 days or advise the claimant of any delay and then continue advising the claimant of the status of the claim every 60 days.

Responding to Problems

Certainly it's possible for you to lose a customer over a service problem that wasn't technically your fault. In most cases, though, you'll find that shippers understand when things go wrong—when drivers do not show up, when equipment breaks down, when crashes occur on the highway, and so on.

What's critical is that you don't ignore problems or try to hide them from your shippers or carriers. Be proactive. When you find out about a problem, make sure everyone who needs to know is notified immediately, and then do everything you can to get the freight back on the road.

Locating and
Setting Up

One of the most appealing aspects of a freight brokerage is that your physical startup requirements are relatively small. Unlike a carrier or freight forwarder, you don't need a warehouse or loading dock. Your customers aren't likely to come to your location, so you don't need to worry about an impressive reception area or elegant offices. In fact, while

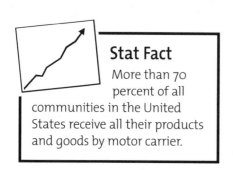

there are some definite advantages to a commercial location, a freight brokerage is an ideal business to start and run from home.

Cathy Davis started MCD Transportation at home but grew enough to move into commercial space just eight months later. Chuck Andrews works from a commercial location in Indianapolis but has agents around the country who work out of their homes. Where you operate depends on your resources and goals for your company. Many brokers start from home with the goal of moving into commercial space as soon as they are established with a few clients, and this is an excellent strategy.

The major benefit of starting a homebased business is the fact that it significantly reduces the amount of startup and initial operating capital you'll need. But there's more to consider than simply the upfront cash. Do you have a separate room for an office, or will you have to work at the dining room table? Can you set up a comfortable workstation with all the tools and equipment you will need? Can you separate your work area from the rest of the house so you can have privacy when you are working—and get away from "the office" when you're not?

You need to be conveniently located so you can personally call on shippers and prospective shippers. If you're planning to hire administrative help, your office needs to be large enough to provide them with adequate work space, and you need available parking.

By contrast, starting in a commercial location requires more initial cash than starting from home. If you decide on this, your range of options is fairly broad, and your choice should be guided largely by the goals you've set for your business in terms of market and growth. Consider office buildings, light industrial parks, and executive suites.

Unless you have an extremely large home, you'll find that a commercial location allows you to create a setup that is more efficient and practical than what you might be able to do in a spare bedroom. Just be careful when shopping for a space. Rental rates and leasing terms vary, so make sure you comparison shop.

Put It In Writing

Whether your goal is a solo homebased operation, a small family business, or a transportation empire, you need to start with a written business plan. This helps you think through what you're doing, see your strengths and weaknesses, and figure out ways to overcome challenges on paper before you have to face them in real life. Writing a business plan is not just a necessary chore; it creates the foundation and sets the vision for your company.

Your business plan should include worst-case scenarios. You'll benefit from thinking ahead about what you'll do if things don't go as you want them to. Think about things such as equipment breakdowns, employees who don't show up (even for valid reasons), uncollectible invoices, and other challenges that are part of doing business today.

For more information on how to write a business plan on which you can build your organization, read the business plan section in *Start Your Own Business* by Rieva Lesonsky (Entrepreneur Press).

The Agent Option

Some brokers may opt to use agents to develop a wider scope of operations. In this context, agents are independent contractors who represent your company in a given area. This enables you to offer a local presence when you may not have the volume to justify opening your own office.

Along these lines, you may want to consider starting out as an agent rather than a broker. Chuck Andrews' company is based in Indianapolis, but he has agents in Texas, Florida, Georgia, West Virginia, and Indiana. Because his agents are not brokers, and because they are homebased, their startup materials are minimal and typically consist of a computer, telephone and fax machine. The agent's work is very similar to what a broker does, but the agent functions under auspices of the broker and the broker is responsible for issues such as paying carriers and maintaining the required surety bonds.

Naming Your Company

Your company name is an important marketing tool. A well-chosen name works very hard for you; choosing an ineffective name means you have to work much harder at marketing your brokerage and letting people know what you have to offer.

Your company name should clearly identify what you do in a way that appeals to your target market. It should be short, catchy, and memorable. It should also be easy to pronounce and spell—people who can't say your company name may use you, but they won't refer anyone else to you.

Cathy Davis gave serious thought to several names before deciding to use her initials. Chuck Andrews chose his company's name—Midwest Freight Brokers Inc.—based on its location and the service the company provides. "We're located in [the Midwest], freight is what we do, and brokers are what we are," he says. Ron Williamson used a combination of his and his wife's initials to come up with RJW Logistics Inc. because he wanted a name no one else was using.

Take a systematic approach to naming your company. Once you've decided on two or three possibilities, take the following steps:

- *Check the name for effectiveness and functionality.* Does it quickly and easily convey what you do? Is it easy to say and spell? Is it memorable in a positive way? Ask several of your friends and associates to serve as a focus group to help you evaluate the name's impact.

- *Search for potential conflicts in your local market.* Find out if any other local or regional business serving your market area has a similar name that might confuse the public.

- *Check for legal availability.* Exactly how you do this depends on the legal structure you choose. Typically, sole proprietorships and partnerships operating under a name other than that of the owner(s) are required by the county, city or state to register their fictitious name. Even if it's not required, it's a good idea because that means no one else can use that name. Sometimes it's as simple as filing for a "doing business as" (dba). Corporations usually operate under their corporate names. In either case, you need to check with the appropriate regulatory agency to be sure the name you choose is available.

- *Check for use on the World Wide Web.* If someone else is already using your name as an address on the World Wide Web, consider coming up with something else. Even if you have no intention of developing a web site of your own, the use of your name by another company could be confusing to your customers.

- *Check to see if the name conflicts with any name listed on your state's trademark register.* Your state Department of Commerce can help you or direct you to the correct agency. You should also check with the trademark register maintained by the U.S. Patent and Trademark Office (PTO).

> **Bright Idea**
> When naming your company, consider creating a word that doesn't exist—that's what companies like Exxon and Kodak did. Just be sure the syllables blend to make an ear-appealing sound and that the name is simple enough for people to remember. Also, make sure you haven't inadvertently come up with a name that means something negative in another language.

Once the name you've chosen passes these tests, you need to protect it by registering it with the appropriate state agency; again, your state Department of Commerce can help you. If you expect to be doing business on a national level, you should also register the name with the PTO.

Choosing a Legal Structure

One of the first decisions you'll need to make about your freight brokerage is the legal structure of your company. This is an important decision. It affects your financial liability, the amount of taxes you pay, and the degree of ultimate control you have over the company. It also affects your ability to attract investors and ultimately sell the business.

Quittin' Time?

Successful freight brokers recommend that you get practical industry experience by working for another broker, carrier or shipper before starting your own enterprise. If you follow that advice, when do you tell your boss about your plans?

There's no one-size-fits-all answer. You need to determine where you stand ethically, legally, and practically. Take any employment-related contracts you have signed—including noncompete and confidentiality agreements—along with your employee handbook—to an attorney. This is especially important if your brokerage will either compete with or use information (such as customer lists) you obtained from your current employer. A lawyer can review those documents, let you know whether or not you are violating the agreements, and help you understand what potential litigation you may face.

Keep in mind that you can be fired for starting your own business. Most states are at-will employment states, which means you can be terminated for any reason or no reason, as long as there is no discrimination involved.

What about trying to start something on the side and building it as long as you can while still working full time? The risk you're taking there, says Cherry Hill, New Jersey, freight broker Bill Tucker, is the image you're projecting to your customers. If you're sneaking around behind your employer's back and violating your employment contract, you're sending a message of questionable judgment and ethics to your customers and associates.

Of course, it's entirely possible that your employer will support your venture. If, for example, you are a sales rep for a carrier, you can present your brokerage business as an opportunity for your employer. You'll still be out there drumming up business for the carrier, and other carriers as well, but you'll be doing it on a commission basis, which means the carrier will no longer have to pay the expenses associated with having you as an employee. "You can sell the partnership idea to the owner of a trucking company," Tucker says. "I know that's been done a lot of times. More and more creative relationships are open for consideration."

However, legal structure shouldn't be confused with operating structure. Attorney Robert S. Bernstein, managing partner with Bernstein Bernstein Krawec & Wymard, P.C., in Pittsburgh, explains the difference: "The legal structure is the ownership structure—who actually owns the company. The operating structure defines who makes management decisions and runs the company."

A sole proprietorship is owned by the proprietor; a partnership is owned by the partners; and a corporation is owned by the shareholders. Another business structure, the limited liability company (LLC), combines the tax advantages of a sole proprietorship with the liability protection of a corporation. The rules on LLCs vary by state; check with your state's Department of Corporations for the latest requirements.

Sole proprietorships and partnerships can be operated however the owners choose. In a corporation, the shareholders typically elect directors who, in turn, elect officers who then employ other people to run and work in the company. But it's entirely possible for a corporation to have only one shareholder and to essentially function as a sole proprietorship. In any case, how you plan to operate the company should not be a major factor in your choice of legal structures.

So what goes into choosing a legal structure? The first point, says Bernstein, is who is actually making the decision on the legal structure. If you're starting the company by yourself, you don't need to take anyone else's preferences into consideration. "But if there are multiple people involved, you need to consider how you're going to relate to each other in the business," he says. "You also need to consider the issue of asset protection and limiting your liability in the event things don't go well."

Something else to think about is your target customers and what their perception will be of your structure. Bernstein says, "There is a tendency to believe that the legal form of a business has some relationship to the sophistication of the owners, with the sole proprietor as the least and the corporation as the most sophisticated." Because your target market is going to be other businesses large enough to be shipping substantial amounts of cargo, it will probably enhance your image if you incorporate.

Your image notwithstanding, the biggest advantage of forming a corporation is in the area of asset protection, which, Bernstein says, is the process of making sure that the assets you don't want to put into the business don't stand liable for business debt. However, to take advantage of the protection a corporation offers, you must respect the corporation's identity. That means maintaining the corporation as a separate entity; keeping your corporate and personal funds separate, even if you are the sole shareholder; and following your state's rules regarding holding annual meetings and other record-keeping requirements.

Davis incorporated based on the advice of both her accountant and attorney; the C corporation suited her operation best for both tax and liability purposes. Andrews is incorporated, but he personally owns 100 percent of the stock, so he can essentially function with the autonomy of a sole proprietor.

You don't need an attorney to set up a corporation, LLC, or partnership. Bernstein says there are plenty of good do-it-yourself books and kits on the market, and most of the state agencies that oversee corporations have guidelines you can use. Even so, it's always a good idea to have a lawyer at least look over your documents before you file them, just to make sure they are complete and will allow you to truly function as you want.

Finally, remember that your choice of legal structure is not an irrevocable decision, although if you're going to make a switch, it's easier to go from the simpler forms to the more sophisticated ones than vice versa. Bernstein says the typical pattern is to start as a sole proprietor and then move up to a corporation as the business grows. But if you need the asset protection of a corporation from the beginning, start out that way. Says Bernstein, "If you're going to the trouble of starting a business, decide on a structure and put it all together; it's worth the extra effort to make sure it's really going to work." For more information on business structure, check out *Start Your Own Business*.

Insurance

Because you never actually take possession of your customers' goods, you don't need to worry about insuring them. It is carriers' responsibility to provide coverage for the value of the freight they are hauling. Generally, a certain amount of value (which may vary by carrier) is calculated into the basic freight rate, and if the actual value of the goods exceeds what the basic rate covers, the shipper can purchase additional protection from the trucking company.

Even though you don't need to worry about insuring freight, your company still has insurance issues to address. If you're homebased, do not assume your homeowner's or renter's policy covers your business equipment; chances are, it doesn't. If you're located in a commercial facility, be prepared for your landlord to require proof of certain levels of liability insurance when you sign the lease. In either case, you need coverage for your equipment and supplies, and workers' compensation if you have employees.

> **Bright Idea**
>
> Sit down with your insurance agent every year and review your insurance needs, which are sure to change as your company grows. Also, insurance companies are always developing new products to meet the needs of the growing small-business market, and it's possible one of these new policies will be more appropriate for you.

A smart approach to insurance is to find an agent who works with other freight brokers and transportation companies. The agent should be willing to help you analyze your needs, evaluate what risks you're willing to accept and what risks you need to insure against, and work with you to keep your insurance costs down.

Typically, homebased freight brokers want to make sure their equipment and supplies are covered against theft and damage by an act of God, such as fire or flood, and that they have some liability protection if someone (a customer, supplier, or employee) is injured on their property. In most cases, one of the new insurance products designed for homebased businesses will provide sufficient coverage. Also, you will probably use your vehicle for business purposes, so make sure it is adequately covered.

If you opt for a commercial location, you'll need to meet the landlord's requirements for general liability coverage. You'll also want to cover your supplies, equipment

Smart Tip

When you purchase insurance on your equipment and fixtures, ask what documentation the insurance company requires before you ever have to file a claim. That way, you'll be sure to maintain appropriate records, and the claims process will be easier.

and fixtures. Once your business is up and running, consider business interruption insurance to replace lost revenue and cover related costs if you are ever unable to operate due to covered circumstances.

You may also want to carry contingency cargo insurance. This is coverage that would take over on cargo if the carrier's insurance did not fully cover the value of a load that was damaged or destroyed.

For more on business insurance, check out the business insurance section in *Start Your Own Business* (Entrepreneur Press).

Professional Advisors

As a business owner, you may be the boss, but you can't be expected to know everything. You will occasionally need to turn to professionals for information and assistance. It's a good idea to establish a relationship with these professionals before you get into a crisis situation.

To shop for a professional service provider, ask friends and associates for recommendations. You might also check with your local chamber of commerce or trade association for referrals. Find someone who understands transportation in general and the brokerage side of it specifically, and appears eager to work with you. Check them out with the Better Business Bureau and the appropriate state licensing agency before committing yourself.

The professional service providers you are likely to need include:

- *Attorney.* You need a lawyer who understands and practices in the area of business and transportation law, who is honest, and who appreciates your patronage. In most parts of the United States, there are many lawyers willing to compete fiercely for the privilege of serving you. Interview several and choose one you feel comfortable with. Be sure to clarify the fee schedule ahead of time, and get your agreement in writing. Keep in mind that good commercial lawyers don't come cheap; if you want good advice, you must be willing to pay for it. Your attorney should review all contracts, leases, letters of intent, and other legal documents before you sign them. They can also help you with collecting bad debts and establishing personnel policies and procedures. Of course, if you are unsure of the legal ramifications of any situation, call your attorney immediately.

- *Accountant.* Among your outside advisors, your accountant is likely to have the greatest impact on the success or failure of your business. If you are forming a corporation, your accountant should counsel you on tax issues during start-up. On an ongoing basis, your accountant can help you organize the statistical data concerning your business, assist in charting future actions based on past performance, and advise you on your overall financial strategy regarding purchasing, capital investment, and other matters related to your business goals. A good accountant also serves as a tax advisor, not only making sure you are in compliance with all applicable regulations, but also that you don't overpay any taxes.

- *Insurance agent.* A good independent insurance agent can assist you with all aspects of your business insurance, from general liability to employee benefits, and probably even handle your personal lines as well. Look for an agent who works with a wide range of insurers and understands your particular business. This agent should be willing to explain the details of various types of coverage, to consult with you to determine the most appropriate coverage, to help you understand the degree of risk you are taking, to work with you to develop risk-reduction programs, and to assist in expediting any claims.

- *Banker.* You need a business bank account and a relationship with a banker. Don't just choose the bank you've always done your personal banking with; it may not be the best bank for your business. Interview several bankers before deciding where to place your business. Once your account is open, maintain a relationship with the banker. Periodically sit down and review your accounts and the services you use to make sure you have the most appropriate package for your situation.

- *Consultants.* The consulting industry is booming—and for good reason. Consultants can provide valuable, objective input on all aspects of your business. (Keep in mind that, as a broker, you will occasionally put on a consultant's hat as you work with your customers.) Consider hiring a business consultant to evaluate your business plan or a marketing consultant to assist you in that area. When you're ready to hire employees, a human resources consultant may help you avoid some costly mistakes. Many freight brokerages are family businesses, so it might help to consult with an expert in the areas of both family dynamics in business and succession planning. For example, after her death, Cathy Davis's daughter, Donna J. Wood, took over as president (she had served as vice president), and her sister, Dionne R. Kegley, became vice president of the Smyrna, Tennessee-based company. Davis had worked diligently to create a succession plan that

> ### Fun Fact
> In 1900, the fuel costs per ton mile for moving freight by horse-drawn vehicles were more than for moving freight by motorized trucks; also, horses required special care in the extreme temperatures of the winter and summer months.

provided for a smooth transition when it became necessary. Consulting fees vary widely, depending on the individual's experience, location, and field of expertise. If you can't afford to hire a consultant, consider contacting the business school at the nearest college or university and hiring an MBA student to help you.

- *Computer expert.* Your computer is your most valuable physical asset, so if you don't know much about computers, find someone to help

you select a system and the appropriate software—someone who will be available to help you maintain, trouble-shoot, and expand your system as you need it.

> **Stat Fact**
> Trucks account for less than 7 percent of all vehicle miles on U.S. roads and highways, yet they pay 35 percent of the total federal highway user taxes.

In addition to your "live" professional advisors, you'll need a collection of resource and reference materials. The freight broker business is full of details so numerous that you can't possibly expect to remember them all. You will need broker and carrier directories, a mileage guide, and business directories. A listing of publications appears in the Appendix.

Create Your Own Advisory Board

Not even the president of the United States is expected to know everything. That's why he surrounds himself with advisors—experts in particular areas who provide knowledge and information to help him make decisions. Savvy small-business owners use a similar strategy.

You can assemble a team of volunteer advisors to meet with you periodically to offer advice and direction. Because this isn't an official or legal entity, you have a great deal of latitude in how you set it up. Advisory boards can be structured to help with the direct operation of your company and to keep you informed on various business, legal, and financial trends that may affect you. Use these tips to set up your advisory board:

- *Structure a board that meets your needs.* Generally, you'll want a legal advisor, an accountant, a marketing expert, a human resources person, and perhaps a financial advisor. You may also want successful entrepreneurs from other industries who understand the basics of business and will view your operation with a fresh eye.

- *Ask the most successful people you can find, even if you don't know them well.* You'll be surprised at how willing people are to help another business succeed.

- *Be clear about what you are trying to do.* Let your prospective advisors know what your goals are and that you don't expect them to take on an active management role or to assume any liability for your company or for the advice they offer.

- *Don't worry about compensation.* Advisory board members are rarely compensated with more than lunch or dinner. Of course, if a member of your board provides a direct service—for example, if an attorney reviews a contract or an accountant prepares a financial statement—then they should be paid at their normal rate. But that's not part of their job as an advisory board member. Keep in mind that, even though you don't write them a check, your advisory board members will likely benefit in a variety of tangible and non-tangible ways. Being on your board will expose them to ideas and perspectives they may not otherwise see and will also expand their own network.

Beware!
Although multi-function devices—such as a copier/printer/fax machine or a fax/telephone/answering machine—may cost less initially and take up less space in your office than stand-alone items, you'll lose all of these functions simultaneously if the equipment fails. Also, consider the machine's efficiency rating and cost to operate; compare that with stand-alone items before buying. However, these machines are more reliable than ever, so one could be right for you.

- *Consider the group dynamics when holding meetings.* You may want to meet with all the members together or in small groups of one or two. It all depends on how they relate to each other and what you need to accomplish.

- *Ask for honesty, and don't be offended when you get it.* Your pride might be hurt when someone points out something you're doing wrong, but the awareness will be beneficial in the long run.

- *Learn from failure as well as success.* Encourage board members to tell you about their mistakes so you can avoid making them.

- *Respect the contribution your board members are making.* Let them know you appreciate how busy they are, and don't abuse or waste their time.

- *Make it fun.* You are, after all, asking these people to donate their time, so create a pleasant atmosphere.

- *Listen to every piece of advice.* Stop talking and listen. You don't have to follow every piece of advice, but you need to hear it.

- *Provide feedback to the board.* Good or bad, let the board know what you did and what the results were.

Basic Office Equipment

As tempting as it may be to fill up your office with an abundance of clever gadgets designed to make your working life easier and more fun, you're better off disciplining yourself to buy only what you need. Consider these basic items:

▲

- *Typewriter.* You may think that most typewriters are in museums these days, but they actually remain quite useful to businesses that deal frequently with pre-printed and multipart forms, such as contracts and shipping documents. A good electric typewriter can be purchased for $100 to $150.

- *Computer and printer.* A computer is an essential piece of equipment for a freight brokerage. It will help you schedule shipments, calculate rates, maintain customer records, handle the financial side of your business, and produce marketing materials. You do not necessarily need the "latest and greatest" in computer power, but at a minimum, you should have a system with a Pentium-class processor, the most current version of Windows, 64MB RAM, 8GB to 10GB hard drive (or larger), CD-ROM drive, 56 Kbps modem, and video card.

- *Software.* Think of software as your computer's brains, the instructions that tell your computer how to accomplish the functions you need. There are many programs on the market that will handle your accounting, customer information management, and other administrative requirements. You'll also want to take a look at the programs designed specifically for freight brokers. Software can be a significant investment, so do a careful analysis of your needs and then study the market and examine a variety of products before making a final decision.

- *Modem.* Modems are necessary to access online services and the internet and have become a standard component of most computers. If you are going to conduct

Something Old, Something New

Should you buy all new equipment, or will used equipment suffice? That depends, of course, on which equipment you're thinking about.

For office furniture (desks, chairs, filing cabinets, bookshelves, etc.), you can get some great deals buying used items. Remember, few people are ever likely to see your office, so make your choices based on functionality rather than appearance. You might also be able to save a significant amount of money buying certain office equipment used, such as your copier, phone system and fax machine. However, for technology-based items, such as your computer, you'll probably be better off buying new. Don't try to run your company on outdated technology.

To find good used equipment, you'll need to shop around. Check out used office furniture and equipment dealers. Also check the classified section of your local paper under items for sale, as well as notices of bankrupt companies and companies that are going out of business.

any business online, whether it's tracking shipments, creating your own web site, doing research, or simply communicating via e-mail, you must have a modem. Depending on your own needs and preferences, you'll have to decide whether you want a basic telephone line modem (that probably comes standard with your computer), a cable modem (about $200 for the hardware and $100 to install), a DSL modem ($200 to $500), or an ISDN modem (about $250 for the hardware and $200 for setup). With the pace of business moving ever faster, you aren't likely to have time to wait for a telephone dial-up modem to do whatever you need online; consider investing in DSL or a cable modem for quicker, more efficient operations.

Bright Idea

Postage stamps come in a wide array of sizes, designs, and themes, and can add elements of color, whimsy and even thoughtfulness to mail. Stamps look more personal; metered mail looks more "corporate." Consider using metered mail for invoices, statements, and other "official" business, and stamps for thank-you notes and similar marketing correspondence that could use an extra personal touch.

- *Data and equipment protection.* You need an uninterruptible power supply to keep your computer from going down in the event of a power failure or brownout, as well as a surge protector to protect your system from power surges. You can buy these items separately or as a combined unit. You'll also need a data backup system that allows you to copy the information from your computer to another location for safe storage.

- *Photocopier.* The photocopier is a fixture of the modern office and is necessary for even the smallest freight brokerage. You can get a basic, low-end, no-frills personal copier for less than $400 in just about any office supply store. More elaborate models increase proportionally in price. If you anticipate a heavy volume, consider leasing.

- *Fax machine.* Fax capability has become another must in modern offices. You can either add a fax card to your computer or buy a stand-alone machine. If you use your computer, it must be able to send or receive faxes, and the transmission may interrupt other work. For most businesses, a stand-alone machine on a dedicated telephone line is a wise investment. Expect to pay $100 to $250 for a fax machine. Be sure to check out the cost of toner or ink and paper before purchasing your fax machine.

- *Postage scale.* Unless all your mail is identical, a postage scale is a valuable investment. An accurate scale takes the guesswork out of postage and will quickly pay for itself. It's a good idea to weigh every piece of mail to eliminate the risk of items being returned for insufficient postage or overpaying when you're unsure of the weight. Light mailers—one to 12 articles per day—will be adequately served by inexpensive mechanical postal scales, which typically range from $10 to $25. If you are averaging 12 to 24 items per day, consider a digital scale, which is somewhat more expensive—generally from $50 to $200—but significantly more accurate than a mechanical unit. If you send more than 24 items per day or use priority or expedited services frequently, invest in an electronic computing scale, which weighs the item and then calculates the rate via the carrier of your choice, making it easy for you to make comparisons. Programmable electronic scales range from $80 to $250.

- *Postage meter.* Postage meters allow you to pay for postage in advance and print the exact amount on the mailing piece when it is used. Many postage meters can print in increments of one-tenth of a cent, which can add up to big savings for bulk mail users. Meters also provide a "big company" professional image, are more convenient than stamps, and can save you money in a number of ways. Postage meters are leased, not sold, with rates starting at about $30 per month. They require a license, which is available from your local post office. Only four manufacturers are licensed by the United States Postal Service to manufacture and lease postage meters; your local post office can provide you with contact information.

- *Paper shredder.* A response to both a growing concern for privacy and the need to recycle and conserve space in landfills, shredders are becoming increasingly common in both homes and offices. They allow you to efficiently destroy incoming unsolicited direct mail, as well as sensitive internal documents before they are discarded. Shredded paper can be compacted much more tightly than paper tossed in a wastebasket, which conserves landfill space. Light-duty shredders start at about $25, and heavier-capacity shredders run $150 to $500.

Telecommunications

The ability to communicate quickly with your customers and suppliers is essential to any business. Also, being able to reach your employees when they are out on jobs is important. Advancing technology gives you a wide range of telecommunications options. Most telephone companies have created departments dedicated to small and homebased businesses. Contact your local service provider and ask to speak with someone who can review your needs and help you put together a service and equipment package that will work for you. Specific elements to keep in mind include:

Telephone

Whether you're homebased or in a commercial location, a single voice telephone line should be adequate during the startup period. As you grow and your call volume increases, you'll add more lines.

Your telephone can be a tremendous productivity tool, and most of the models on the market today are rich in features you will find useful. Such features include automatic redial, which redials the last number called at regular intervals until the call is completed; programmable memory for storing frequently called numbers; and speakerphone for hands-free use. You may also want call forwarding, which allows you to forward calls to another number when you are not at your desk, and call waiting, which signals you that another call is coming in while you are on the phone. These services are typically available through your telephone company for a monthly fee.

If you're going to be spending a great deal of time on the phone, perhaps doing marketing or handling customer service, consider a headset for comfort and efficiency. A cordless phone lets you move around freely while talking, but these units vary widely in price and quality, so research them thoroughly before making a purchase.

Look into the possibility of a startup package of options to save money.

- *Answering machine/voice mail.* Because your business phone should never go unanswered, you need some sort of reliable answering device to take calls when you can't do it yourself. Whether you buy an answering machine (expect to pay $40 to $150 for one that is suitable for a business) or use the voice-mail service provided through your telephone company (anywhere from $6 to $20 per month) depends on your personal preferences, work style, and needs.

- *Cellular phone.* Once considered a luxury, cellular phones have become standard equipment not only for businesspeople, but for just about everyone. Most have features similar to your office phone—such as caller ID, call waiting, and voice mail—and equipment and services packages are very reasonably priced. Features such as digital images, text messaging, e-mail, news services, and more are becoming increasingly available and affordable. Be sure to set policies for employees who will be using cellular phones.

- *Pager.* A pager lets you know that someone is trying to reach you and allows you to decide when to return the call. Many people use pagers in conjunction with cellular phones to conserve the cost of air time. Ask prospective pager suppliers if your system can be set up so you are paged whenever someone leaves a message in your voice-mail box; this service allows you to retrieve your messages immediately and eliminates having to periodically check to see if anyone has called. As with cellular phones, the pager industry is very competitive, so shop around for the best deal.

- *Toll-free number.* Even if most of your shippers are local, it's highly unlikely that all of their customers will be, too. You'll want to provide nonlocal shippers, consignees, and trucking companies and their drivers with a toll-free number so they can reach you without having to make a long-distance call. Most long-distance service providers offer toll-free numbers, and they have a wide range of service and price packages. Shop around to find the best deal for you.

- *E-Mail.* E-mail is rapidly becoming a standard element in a company's communication package. It allows for fast, efficient, trackable 24-hour communication. Check your messages regularly and reply to them promptly.

Keep Your Customers Out of Voice-Mail Jail

Voice mail is one of the most popular modern business conveniences and can be an efficient communication tool. But keep in mind that the pace of the freight industry is so rapid that there isn't always time to return calls, so whenever possible, answer your phone yourself—and insist that your employees do likewise—and handle calls as quickly and smoothly as possible.

Some other telephone tips:

- If you use an automated answering system, be sure to tell callers how to reach a live person. Ideally, that information should come very early in your announcement. For example, your greeting might sound something like this:

    Thank you for calling ABC Freight Brokers. If you know the extension of the person you are calling, you may enter it now. To reach an operator, dial zero at any time during this message. For dispatch, press one. For tracing, press two. For billing, press three. For a company directory, press four.

- Whether you're a one-person show or you have a sizable staff, change your individual voice-mail announcements daily. Callers need to know whether you're in the office or out and whether they're likely to hear back from you in five minutes or five hours. Avoid saying the obvious, such as "I'm either away from my desk or out of the office." If you were at your desk, you would be answering your phone. And always let callers know how to reach a live person when you're not available. Here's a sample individual voice-mail announcement:

    This is Jane Smith, and it's Monday, June 1. I'm in the office today but unavailable at the moment. Leave your name, number and the reason for your call, and I'll get back to you within an hour. If you need to speak to someone immediately, press zero and ask the operator to connect you with Bob White.

Transportation Brokerage Software

Technology has made starting a freight brokerage easier than ever, and there are several software packages on the market designed specifically for brokers. See the Appendix for a partial list of resources. In addition, you can get off-the-shelf word processors, spreadsheets, accounting programs, and other software functions to help you run your business.

"By spending money upfront on computer and communication technology, you are saving money in the long run," says Cherry Hill, New Jersey, freight broker Bill Tucker. "You'll also have a lot more sales appeal with the ability to provide information to customers."

Inventory

Because the only thing you sell is service, you'll require very little in the way of inventory—but what you do need to keep on hand is important.

You'll need to be sure to maintain an adequate stock of marketing materials, including brochures, sales items, etc. You'll also need to maintain an ample supply of administrative items, including checks, invoices, stationery, paper and miscellaneous office supplies. Use the "Office Supplies Checklist" on page 57 to make sure you haven't forgotten anything. Using the checklist will also help you estimate your startup costs.

Company Vehicle

Though you won't be hauling freight yourself, you will do a substantial amount of interacting with your customers at their places of business, and you'll meet with truckers at their terminals and offices. You will also need to attend various professional and networking functions. You can either use your own vehicle or have your company purchase or lease a vehicle that you use for business.

Because you may have customers and/or colleagues riding with you, choose a four-door sedan-type vehicle that is roomy and comfortable. It should also have a sizable trunk so you have plenty of space to carry files and supplies (and a set of golf clubs, if you play).

Remember that your automobile is essentially your mobile office, and you will be judged by its appearance. Keep it clean, both inside and out. Wash it regularly to avoid a buildup of road grime, and do not allow trash and papers to accumulate inside. If you smoke, empty the ashtray daily and use a deodorizer for the comfort of your nonsmoking passengers. (Sure, it's your car, and if you want to smoke, that's your business, but remember that buying decisions are often based on emotional factors, then later justified with logic and reason. A nonsmoker who is offended by a smoker will find a way to avoid doing business with that person.)

Office Supplies Checklist

Use this handy list as a shopping guide for equipping your office with supplies (you probably already have some of these). After you've done your shopping, fill in the purchase price next to each item, add up your costs, and you'll have a head start on estimating your start-up costs.

❑ Scratch pads $ _____

❑ Staplers, staples, and staple removers $ _____

❑ Tape and dispensers $ _____

❑ Scissors $ _____

❑ "Sticky" notes in an assortment of sizes $ _____

❑ Paper clips $ _____

❑ Plain paper and toner for your copier and printer $ _____

❑ Paper and other supplies for your fax machine $ _____

❑ Letter openers $ _____

❑ Pens, pencils, and holders $ _____

❑ Correction fluid $ _____
   (to correct typewritten or handwritten documents)

❑ Trash cans $ _____

❑ Desktop document trays $ _____

❑ Labels $ _____

Total office supplies expenditures $ _____

Staffing Your
Company

Y ou can start and run a successful brokerage
as a one-person show, but to really grow, you're going to need
employees. If you find the idea of interviewing, hiring and
managing employees somewhat intimidating, you're not
alone—that's a common feeling among entrepreneurs. But
this is very much a people business, and the people you hire

will be critical to the success of your company, so it's in your best interest to do it carefully and wisely.

When Cathy Davis started MCD Transportation in Smyrna, Tennessee, she was her company's only employee. Today, the business she has passed on to her daughters has five full-time people. When Cherry Hill, New Jersey, freight broker Bill Tucker bought his late father's company, it was staffed by a few part-time retired traffic managers. Today, there are some 30 people on the payroll, plus a few commissioned salespeople who work as independent contractors. "We pride ourselves on realizing that this is a people business," he says. "It's incumbent on us to be able to attract and hold the best people we can."

Ron Williamson started RJW Logistics with himself and his wife working part time. Today, he employs nearly 50 people in his Bloomingdale, Illinois, office, plus about 150 drivers—mostly owner-operators—for his trucking operations.

This chapter discusses some of the hiring issues that are specific to freight brokerages. For more information on screening, interviewing, and hiring personnel, consult *Start Your Own Business* by Rieva Lesonsky (Entrepreneur Press).

Pay scales in the transportation industry are very much affected by geography and market. For example, an experienced dispatcher in Chicago could easily earn

---

Smart Start

Before you set up the first interview with an applicant, lay some groundwork to make the hiring process as smooth as possible.

- ○ *Decide in advance what you need.* You know you need help, but exactly what kind of help? Do you need a salesperson or administrative support? Do you need a broker or someone to handle billing? In the beginning, you'll be looking for people to do the tasks you can't or don't want to do. As you grow, you'll be looking for people who can help you expand your capabilities.

- ○ *Write job descriptions.* Take the time to put a list of responsibilities and required skills in writing. This forces you to think through what type of person will best meet your needs, which reduces the risk of hiring the wrong person, and it gives you something to show applicants so they can tell if the job you are offering is the one they want.

- ○ *Set basic personnel policies.* Don't think that because you're a small company you can just deal with personnel issues as they come up. You'll avoid a lot of problems down the road if you set policies at the outset.

double what the same position would pay in Parkersburg, West Virginia. Another point to consider is that the pool of knowledgeable, experienced people is relatively small, so the wages in this industry will likely be higher than in many other industries. Do some informal networking in your community to determine what the going pay scales and commission ranges are before deciding how much you're going to pay. Whatever you decide to offer in the beginning, from the day they are hired, tell employees what they must do to get a raise without having to ask for it; then follow up by increasing their pay rates when they've earned it.

It's a good idea to hire people before you desperately need them. Waiting until the last minute may drive you to make hiring mistakes, which can cost you dearly, both in terms of cash and customer service.

When you first begin hiring people, you may want to consider bringing them on as part-timers until your business grows to the point that full-timers are required. One of the biggest keys to getting and keeping good people is flexibility, and you will find plenty of talented folks who, for whatever reason, don't want to work full time. If you can accommodate them, you'll both benefit. And as the workload grows and you need a full-time person doing that particular job, either change the status of your part-timer or, if that won't work, be creative. Consider hiring a second part-timer, setting up a job-sharing situation, or some other solution that will allow you to retain a valuable person and still get the work done.

Basic Positions

Because the service you offer is pretty straightforward, you don't need a wide range of job titles in your company. Here are the basic positions you'll need to fill as you grow:

- *Broker.* A broker does the basic tasks that you do. This person needs to understand all the details involved in arranging a shipment and have good communication skills. A background in trucking is helpful. Unless you have a full-time bookkeeper or accountant, you or your brokers will have to bill shippers and pay carriers. You can either pay brokers a salary or a commission based on their sales.
- *Secretary/receptionist.* In most freight brokerages, this individual answers the telephone, routes calls, takes messages (if you don't have voice mail), greets visitors (though they will be infrequent), and handles routine word processing and correspondence.
- *Customer service/account representative.* This is an inside person who handles all customer service duties, including quoting rates, taking pickup orders, tracking shipments, assisting customers with claims, and dealing with any service issues that arise.
- *Bookkeeper.* This individual keeps your financial records and may also handle billing and payables.

- *Sales representative.* A sales rep may work inside on the phone, outside face-to-face or a combination of both. This person's job is to identify and secure new business and help maintain existing business.

Calling all People

Picture the ideal candidate in your mind. Is this person unemployed and reading the classified ads? It's possible, but you'll improve your chances for a successful hire if you are more creative in your search techniques than simply writing a help wanted ad.

Sources for prospective employees include carriers, customers (use caution here; you do not want to lose a client because you stole an employee), and professional associations. Put the word out among your social contacts as well—you never know who else might know the perfect person for your company.

Stat Fact
Demographic projections indicate that finding good employees is going to be one of the biggest challenges all businesses face well into the 21st century.

Evaluating Applicants

When you actually begin the hiring process, don't be surprised if you're as nervous at the prospect of interviewing potential employees as they are about being interviewed. They may need a job, but for you, the future of your company is at stake.

It's a good idea to prepare your interview questions in advance. Develop open-ended questions that encourage the candidate to talk. In addition to knowing what they have done, you want to find out how they did it. Ask each candidate the same set of questions, and take notes as they respond so you can make an accurate assessment and comparison later. If candidates claim to have experience, use industry jargon to see how well they understand it; the freight business has a language of its own that most outsiders won't be able to speak.

Smart Tip

Tip...

Before you hire your first employee, make sure you are prepared. Have all your paperwork ready, know what you need to do in the way of tax reporting, and understand all the liabilities and responsibilities that come with having employees.

When the interview is over, let the candidate know what to expect. Is it going to take you several weeks to interview other candidates, check references, and make a decision? Will you want the top candidates to return for a second interview? Will you call the candidate, or should they call you? This is not only a good business practice; it's also common courtesy.

Always check former employers and personal references. Though many companies are very restrictive as to what information they'll verify, you may be surprised at what you can find out. At least confirm that the applicant told the truth about dates and positions held. Personal references are likely to give you some additional insight into the general character and personality of the candidate; this helps you decide if they'll fit into your operation.

Be sure your employees are legal. Under federal law, you must verify the identity and employment eligibility of employees; complete and retain the Employment Eligibility Verification Form (I-9) on file for at least three years, or one year after employment ends, whichever period of time is longer; and do not discriminate on the basis of national origin and citizenship status.

Be sure to document every step of the interview and reference-checking process. Even very small companies are finding themselves targets of employment discrimination suits; good records are your best defense if it happens to you.

Benefits

Many of the employees you want could be working for major freight carriers or large manufacturers and enjoying "big company" benefits. You can't afford not to offer a strong benefit package. The brokers we spoke with provide paid vacation and holidays, health and life insurance, retirement plans, bonuses, profit-sharing, and flex-time.

As a smaller company, you have a degree of flexibility large companies don't always have. For many people, especially those with children at home or who care for elderly parents, flexible working hours can be a tremendous benefit.

Give your employees subscriptions to industry trade magazines and newsletters, and encourage them to use and share the information they learn from those publications. The cost is nominal, and the result is that you'll increase their value to the company as well as their sense of self-esteem.

> **Tip...**
>
> **Smart Tip**
> Hire people as soon as you start to feel you need them. You may be able to start by yourself, but to really grow and generate substantial revenue and profits, you need a team.

Williamson says that, in addition to tangible benefits, you need to create a pleasant working environment. "This is a high-stress business, and we try to make the job fun," he says.

Keep People in Perspective

There is no business where the slogan "people are our most valuable asset" is more true than in transportation, and taking care of your people is certainly important. But it's also important to keep the relationship of the individual to the company in perspective.

"When you hire people, you can never let them think they are more important than the company," says Indianapolis freight broker Chuck Andrews. When he started his company, he hired a few people who brought business with them; they had an inflated opinion of their value to the company and used that to attempt to manipulate Andrews. Don't give in to this brand of professional blackmail. Of course, it's possible that when you lose certain employees, you may also lose some customers—but it's also possible that you won't, and it's highly unlikely that the loss of one person can destroy your business if you've built it properly.

> **Bright Idea**
> Find out what your employees want in the way of benefits before you spend time and money developing a package. Do a brief survey; ask what they think of the ideas you have and ask for their ideas. If they want something you can't afford to do, don't reject it immediately; figure out what you can afford, and explain the situation to the employee.

Says Andrews, "You have to let employees know they're important to you, but you can't let them think they have you over the rack and can come and go as they want."

The High Cost of Turnover

Employee turnover is an important issue in the transportation industry, especially in sales and customer service positions. Remember, this is a relationship business, and when you have employees who have built strong relationships with customers and carriers, you have employees who will be the constant target of recruiting efforts by other companies.

Some of the costs of turnover are fairly easy to calculate; others are essentially priceless. When someone leaves, you have the hard costs of paying overtime to other employees to get that job done until a replacement is found, of recruiting (advertising, screening, interviewing, etc.), and of training. Those numbers are fairly easy to figure. Harder to calculate is the cost in customer relations and goodwill. You may even lose a few customers who opt to follow the departed employee to a different broker or carrier.

> **Beware!**
> Sometimes small companies lose good employees to larger firms that have better career opportunities. They may not be attracted as much by the money and benefits as they are by the room to grow and advance. Do the best you can to offer career growth to your people.

Bill Tucker says the key to keeping turnover down is to avoid seeing your relationship as an employer-employee one, but rather as partners. That certainly includes bonuses and profit-sharing programs, but it goes beyond pure financial incentives.

Employees need to participate in the decision-making process; they need to be encouraged to contribute ideas and solutions.

People also need to be treated with fairness and compassion. It isn't realistic to expect people to leave their personal lives at home. When employees need you to be flexible about family issues—whether it's taking a few hours off to watch a child perform in a play or needing help dealing with an elderly parent requiring full-time nursing care—it's not only kind but wise for you to provide as much assistance as possible. Along with doing the humane thing, you'll be building a level of employee loyalty that can't be bought for any amount of salary.

Why Train?

Training is an area of managing people that you can't escape. Many of your employees come on board with at least a basic knowledge of the work they must do. But even the most experienced need to be trained in your particular operation and procedures.

The transportation industry has an abundance of training opportunities, from formal courses of study at colleges and universities, to special conventions and workshops, to monthly professional association meetings. It's a good idea to support a variety of training opportunities. For example, MCD Transportation provides both formal and on-the-job training and maintains a company library with current publications. Employees are encouraged to work on their professional certification, and the company pays for related studies. The company also pays for costs related to membership and participation in professional associations.

Credential Potential

Gain additional respect for yourself, your staff, and your company by encouraging your employees to earn the Certified Transportation Broker (CTB) designation. The CTB credential was developed by the Transportation Intermediaries Association (TIA) to increase industry professionalism and integrity through a rigorous program of study and examination. Candidates complete a home-study course designed around academic scholarship and practical experience and then sit for a four-hour proctored exam to earn their credentials. For more information on CTB certification, contact the TIA at (703) 299-5700 or www.tianet.org.

Training Techniques

Whether done in a formal classroom setting or on the job, effective training begins with a clear goal and a plan for reaching it. Training falls into one of three major categories: orientation, which includes explaining company policies and procedures; job skills, which focuses on how to do specific tasks; and ongoing development, which enhances the basic job skills and grooms employees for future challenges and opportunities. These tips will help you maximize your training efforts:

- *Find out how people learn best.* Delivering training is not a one-size-fits-all proposition. People absorb and process information differently, and your training method needs to be compatible with their individual preferences. Some people can read a manual, others prefer a verbal explanation, and still others need to see a demonstration. In a group training situation, your best strategy is to use a combination of methods; when you're working one-on-one, tailor your delivery to fit the needs of the person you're training.

  With some employees, figuring out how they learn best is a simple matter of asking them. Others may not be able to tell you because they don't understand it themselves; in those cases, experiment with various training styles and see what works best for the specific employee.

- *Use simulation and role playing to train, practice, and reinforce.* One of the most effective training techniques is simulation, which involves showing an employee how to do something and then allowing them to practice the technique in a safe, controlled environment. If the task includes interpersonal skills, let the employee role-play with a co-worker to practice what they should say and do in various situations.

- *Be a strong role model.* Don't expect more from your employees than you are willing to do. You're a good role model when you do things the way they should be done all the time. Don't take shortcuts you don't want your employees to take or behave in any way that you don't want them to behave. On the other hand, don't assume that simply doing things the right way is enough to teach others how to do things. Role-modeling is not a substitute for training. It reinforces training. If you only role-model but never train your employees, your employees aren't likely to get the message.

- *Look for training opportunities.* Once you get beyond basic orientation and job skills training, you need to constantly be on the lookout for opportunities to enhance the skill and performance levels of your people.

- *Make it real.* Whenever possible, use real-life situations to train—but avoid letting customers know they've become a training experience for employees.

- *Anticipate questions.* Don't assume that employees know what to ask. In a new situation, people often don't understand enough to formulate questions. Anticipate their questions and answer them in advance.

- *Ask for feedback.* Finally, encourage employees to let you know how you're doing as a trainer. Just as you evaluate their performance, convince them that it's OK to tell you the truth, ask them what they thought of the training and your techniques, and use that information to improve your own skills.

Noncompete Agreements

To protect yourself from an employee leaving you to start his or her own firm that directly competes with yours, you may want to ask everyone who comes to work for you to sign a noncompete agreement. Noncompete agreements typically consist of time, geography, and industry restrictions, and their enforceability varies by state. For example, they are generally illegal in California, but in New York, they are enforceable if the restrictions are "reasonable." Have the language of your noncompete agreement checked by an attorney familiar with employment law before you ask anyone to sign it.

Keep in mind that even though your employees sign noncompete agreements, they may choose to violate them. Then you will have to make the decision whether or not to take the issue to court.

Ron Williamson sued one former employee, a salesperson who started his own company. "We won, but we lost," he says. "It cost me about $32,000, and we settled out of court through arbitration and recovered about $12,000 of that. I had to go to my customers and ask them to testify against this person. Noncompetes are tough, and they take an incredible amount of time [to enforce]."

That may be, but his willingness to sue helped when another former employee left the company. He started to violate the terms of his agreement but backed off when he realized Williamson would take action.

Now that we've covered human resources issues, it's time to discuss marketing.

7

Marketing

Remember in Chapter 1 we said that just about everything must move at least part of the way to its destination by truck? With that in mind, it is safe to say that almost every company is a potential customer for you. But if you take that approach, you'll have a tough time coming up with an effective, not to mention affordable, marketing plan.

What's wrong with just going after anybody in the world who might ever have to ship something by truck for any reason? Because that market segment includes literally millions of companies and individuals, and it's impossible for any small business to communicate effectively with a market that size. Can you afford to send even one piece of direct mail to 1 million prospective customers? Of course not. But when you narrow that market down to, for example, 500 or 1,000 customers in a particular area, conducting a successful direct-mail campaign is much more affordable and manageable.

Keep these questions in mind as you form your marketing plan:

- Who are your potential customers?
- How many of them are there?
- Where are they located?
- How do they currently transport freight?
- Can you offer them anything they are not getting now?
- How can you persuade them to do business with you?
- Exactly what services do you offer?
- How do you compare with your competitors?
- What kind of image do you want to project?

> **Bright Idea**
> One of the most effective ways to build your customer list is word-of-mouth. Provide excellent service to your shippers, and you will increase the likelihood that they'll spread the word about your business to other shippers.

The goal of your marketing plan should be to convey your existence and the quality of your service to prospective customers, ideally using a multifaceted approach. The advertising and marketing section in *Start Your Own Business* (Entrepreneur Press) explains how to create a basic marketing plan.

Market Research

Market research provides businesses with data that allows them to identify and reach particular market segments and to solve or avoid marketing problems. A thorough market survey forms the foundation of any successful business. It is impossible to develop marketing strategies or an effective product line without market research.

The goal of market research is to identify your market, find out where it is, and develop a strategy to communicate with prospective customers in a way that will convince them to use you.

Begin by focusing on two broad areas: the people and firms you work with directly (such as carriers and shippers), and the general business trends that affect the industry as a whole. With this information, you will be able to move on to more specific research that will help you determine your target market, where to locate your business, what services to offer, and your geographic scope of operations.

Choosing a Niche

There are many valid reasons for choosing a well-defined market niche. By targeting a specific market segment, you can tailor your service package and marketing efforts to meet that segment's needs. You'll also develop a reputation for expertise that attracts new customers.

One of the best parts of being a freight broker is that you build long-term relationships with most of your customers. Motor carrier freight service is rarely a one-time purchase; once a customer comes on board with you, you will likely get plenty of repeat business. However, most shippers use multiple carriers and brokers, which means you must take the time to find out as much as you can about shippers' volumes and needs, and provide consistent service so they are comfortable coming back to you, and you can increase your share of their business.

"We become an extension of our customers' management style and/or traffic program," said Smyrna, Tennessee, freight broker Cathy Davis. "We have a much larger carrier base than they do and usually have better negotiation skills, especially if it's a small shipper. We do the calling for them, which frees them to work on other projects. We know how to qualify carriers and have access to more information [about them] than the shipper does."

You can design your niche based on geography (either location of shippers or destination of freight), types of cargo (agricultural, perishable, oversized, bulk commodities, etc.), size of loads, specific industries, or some other special shipping need. To choose a niche, first consider what types of shipments and/or shippers you enjoy working with. Then conduct market research to determine if there is a sufficient demand for the services you want to provide. If there is, move ahead with your marketing plan. If there isn't, consider how you might adjust your niche to one that generates adequate revenue.

Communicating with Your Customers

Once you've selected a niche, you'll need to consider how to let the shippers in that niche know about you; this is the essence of marketing. Don't be discouraged if your marketing efforts don't produce an immediate response. This is a relationship business, and it takes time to build your reputation and the rapport you need with shippers. Also, remember that your marketing efforts support your primary sales efforts but rarely generate a sale on their own. Even so, they deserve your attention.

```
          ┌──────────── Tip...
          │  Smart Tip       ?
          │                  •
          │  Set up an interactive
          │  web site where cus-
          │  tomers can request rate
          │  quotes, and customers and
          │  carriers can contact you for
          │  other information via forms or
          │  e-mail.
          └────────────────────────
```

All your promotional and advertising materials must clearly indicate your status as a broker, must be under the name by which you are registered, and may not directly or indirectly represent your operation as a carrier. With that legal caveat out of the way, be sure all these items are professional and letter-perfect. Consistency is important; your business card, envelopes, stationery, labels, invoices, promotional items, etc., should all have the same logo, use the same typeface, and be on the same color and type of paper (where appropriate, of course—your invoices and stationery will likely be on different stock).

Small but useful giveaway items—such as pens, mugs, scratch pads, and baseball caps—are very effective in supporting your marketing efforts. Customers aren't likely to choose a broker based on these items, but it's important to keep your name in front of them in a positive way. Be sure they clearly and consistently identify your company and tell how to contact you.

Your Yellow Pages listing is important so shippers can find you. Check with your local phone company to find out its advertising deadline and directory distribution date, and, if possible, plan to launch your business in time to be included. For most freight brokers, a Yellow Pages display ad will not be worth the substantial investment that goes along with it; however, you might want to give your listing some distinction by having it set in bold type or including a line or two indicating your specialties or market niche.

Broadcast (radio and television) advertising is generally not effective for freight brokers, but some print advertising will help build your credibility and name recognition. Look for publications that shippers in your target market read; if you're not sure what they are, ask some of the shippers you'd like to have as customers. Your ads do not have to be wildly creative; in fact, a better approach is to simply say what you do and why you do it well in an abbreviated format and then include your company name, your logo, and how to contact you. Keep the design of the ad clear and uncluttered; don't cram so much text into it that no one will read it. Some great places to begin your print advertising are in the newsletters of your local transportation organizations.

You will also want a brochure that describes what you do. A basic 8.5-by-11-inch three-panel piece is sufficient. It should include your company name, address, phone, and fax numbers; web site and e-mail addresses and other contact information; your logo; a detailed list of the services you provide; a brief description of your background to establish credibility; and a benefits statement that tells shippers why they should use you.

Use a professional graphic designer and copywriter to produce your ads and brochures, and have them reproduced by quality offset printing. Don't just run them off on your laser printer or a photocopy machine; your prospective customers will be able to tell, and you'll look like an unstable, fly-by-night operation.

Know Thine Enemy

One of the most basic elements of effective marketing is differentiating yourself from the competition. One marketing consultant calls it "eliminating the competition," because if no one else does exactly what you do, then you essentially have no competition. However, before you can differentiate yourself, you first need to understand who your competitors are, and why your customers might use them.

As a freight broker, you'll be competing with other brokers, freight forwarders, carriers, and probably some types of transportation consulting firms. To a degree, you'll also be competing with your customers' internal traffic departments.

Finding out about your competitors isn't difficult. In many cases, you'll know their people from your own industry networking, perhaps from previous jobs or professional associations. Your customers and potential customers will usually be very open about what they like and don't like about other service providers. The key is to pay attention, take notes, and use what you learn in your own marketing efforts.

Outsourcing Opportunity

As you plan your marketing strategy, consider how the trend of outsourcing can help your brokerage. Outsourcing is the practice of contracting with an outside firm to handle tasks that are not part of a company's core business. For example, as a freight broker, your core business is to link shippers and carriers, so you may choose to outsource such tasks as certain accounting procedures, some of your marketing functions, or perhaps the technical work involved in building a web site.

Many companies are outsourcing all or part of their shipping functions. Brokers are in an excellent position to offer themselves as an outsourcing resource, essentially functioning as the customer's traffic department. You can relieve your customers of all the work related to transportation and traffic management, and in addition, save them money and improve their service.

"A number of our smaller customers use us for their entire shipping and receiving business," says Bill Tucker in Cherry Hill, New Jersey. "Not only on

> **Bright Idea**
>
> Establish yourself as an expert by writing articles for transportation trade publications, as well as the trade publications your target market reads. If you don't have the writing skills and/or the time to compose articles yourself, hire a professional writer to ghostwrite (write under your name) them for you.

the traffic management but also some of the purchasing and acquiring of products." This type of consulting service does not require any particular license—just knowledge and the ability to provide the service.

Of course, it's not a good idea to go to the traffic manager and pitch yourself as a supplier who wants to take over his job. You'll have a much better chance of succeeding if you approach a senior person in the organization whose interest is finance, such as the CFO.

"You may go in and try to eliminate the traffic manager's job," says Chuck Andrews in Indianapolis. "[Try to] convince the vice president of finance or the president of the company that by using your service, he can do away with one person. If [you are talking about] a traffic manager who is wearing multiple hats, [your sales position is that] you are there to assist him and make his job easier."

Join the Right Groups

Professional associations offer a variety of networking and educational opportunities. If you're serious about being a freight broker, you'll belong to several organizations, some industry-exclusive and others more general.

Some of the associations you may consider include (see the Appendix for contact information):

- Transportation Intermediaries Association
- Delta Nu Alpha
- National Association of Small Trucking Companies
- National Association of Women Business Owners (for women-owned brokerage firms)
- Local transportation and traffic clubs
- Your local chamber of commerce
- A lead exchange or small local networking group

It's a good idea to belong to the local transportation clubs in all the cities in which you do business. For example, Andrews belongs to three transportation associations in Indianapolis where his company has its headquarters, plus clubs in Chicago, Cincinnati, and other major areas where he does business. He doesn't attend every single meeting, but he goes to the ones he can, and his name and company are listed on the membership rosters. "We get phone calls out of the blue from people who see our name on those rosters," he says.

Done correctly, marketing can really give your business a boost—especially in the beginning, when you need it most. Now . . . on to sales.

Sales

The freight industry involves the buying and selling of an intangible service, which makes it a strong "relationship" business. Success as a freight broker requires that you do a tremendous amount of both face-to-face and telephone sales.

Don't let the word "selling" scare you. Most of the world's top sales professionals will tell you they hate "selling." What they mean is, they hate the vision of the slick, fast-talking character on the used car lot or the door-to-door peddler who wedges a foot in the door and won't leave until you buy. But that's not "selling" in the professional sense of the word.

When you sell as a freight broker, you convince shippers that you have the capability to help them with their shipping needs better than anyone else—and if you don't believe that, then you need to be in another business. You are not going to browbeat them into using you, nor are you going to manipulate them into buying a service they don't need. You're going to provide the best professional service that meets their needs at a competitive rate, and communicating that is a major part of the sales process.

Phone or Face-to-Face Sales

You might hate the telemarketers who call your home at precisely the moment you are sitting down to dinner, but when it comes to selling your own service, a telephone call can be a very powerful tool. RJW Logistics has a sales rep who generates $2 million a year in gross revenue just by calling people on the phone.

The transportation industry used to be very much a "good old boy" system of casual, drop-in sales calls that consisted primarily of telling a few jokes, leaving behind some scratch pads, and asking for a shipment by saying something like, "Got anything going my way?" Today's transportation professionals don't have time for unexpected visitors with no clear agenda. Collectively, they're spending billions of dollars each year to move materials, and they need those goods to arrive on time, in good condition, at a reasonable and competitive price.

This is not to say that you shouldn't be friendly and personable—in fact, your personality plays an important role in the growth of your business. But each sales contact should have a clear purpose that ultimately provides a benefit to your customer. Most customers appreciate a systematic, sophisticated approach that doesn't waste their time.

In today's intensely competitive environment, the majority of brokers mix telephone and face-to-face sales, using the phone to pre-qualify and set appointments, making a personal call, and then following up on the phone and by mail.

Qualifying Prospects

The first step of the sales process is qualifying the prospect, which is sales training jargon for determining how much business the potential customer has and who makes the decision as to who is going to get it.

> ## ⚠ Beware!
>
> Be careful that you don't patronize or insult the support staff of your customers or prospective customers. Keep in mind that these people may not only influence the decision-making process, but they may eventually be promoted to decision-making positions—either with that company or another one. So treat them with respect, be concerned about their needs and nurture a professional relationship with them.

This is not as hard as it seems. It really involves asking a few simple questions. If you networked your way into the company, you probably have a pretty good idea of the answers. If you're cold-calling, simply ask the receptionist or operator "Can you give me the name and title of the person in charge of choosing carriers for your outbound shipments?"

It is important to ask for both the name and the title before you ask to be connected with that individual. Of course, sometimes operators will transfer your call, but when they don't, you begin the conversation with the advantage of knowing whom you're talking to and the ability to call that person by name.

Once you're on the phone with that person, confirm that you are indeed talking to the decision maker. The receptionist may have referred you to the shipping clerk, who fills out the freight bills, calls carriers, and handles some tracing functions—but who does not actually make the decisions. Don't be shy about asking this question. Most companies these days operate "lean and mean," and workers don't have time to listen to a sales presentation they don't have the authority to act on.

As we've said, you need to identify the real decision maker (and keep in mind that there may be more than one in many companies), but don't ignore the decision influencers. As the name indicates, these are the people who are in a position to influence the decision-making process. They could be telephone operators, receptionists, administrative workers, shipping and receiving clerks—even high-ranking corporate officers.

Think about this: Say you and another broker are competing for a major piece of business from a particular company. The plant manager is making the decision, and his goal is to find someone who can work well with his shipping clerk so he can delegate the details and focus on other things. You and the other broker are offering very similar rate and service packages, but the other broker took the time to talk with the shipping clerk, maybe even took him to lunch, and established a relationship you don't have. With all else being nearly equal, if the plant manager asks the shipping clerk for input in the decision, who do you think he's going to recommend?

This doesn't mean you need to wine and dine every shipping clerk at every company you deal with, or that you need to send all the receptionists flowers and candy every week. What it means is that you respect their roles in the process and you communicate with them to find out what they need and how you can best meet those needs.

Determining Needs

Once you've confirmed that a business has freight you can handle, and you know who makes the routing decisions, you need to find out what they need before you begin telling them what you can do. It's a waste of their time and yours for you to do this any other way. For example, why bother to spend time telling them about the wide variety of equipment you can provide only to find out 20 minutes later that they only need standard trailers? Besides wasting time, that sends a clear message that you're far more interested in making the sale than you are in your customer.

So how do you find out what a prospective customer needs? Simple: Just ask. Say something like "Before I tell you about our services, I'd like to ask you a few questions and find out exactly what you need. Can you tell me about your outbound freight?" Most of the time, you'll get more information than you need. Have a notebook handy and take notes while your customer talks; don't count on being able to accurately remember all the details of weights, commodities, and destinations. Most importantly, never say "no" to a customer. When they need something you can't provide, offer them an alternative instead.

> **Tip...**
>
> ## Smart Tip
>
> Before your first sales calls, do some research on the companies so you know how to approach them. Find out what they do, what they ship and who the decision makers are. Are they senior executives looking to improve service and save money, or a traffic manager who will see you as a threat? "If you go in the wrong way, you're dead in the water," says Indianapolis freight broker Chuck Andrews.

Why Do You Ask?

When a customer (or a prospect) asks you a question about your capabilities, find out what's behind the question before you answer it. This lets you answer in the most positive and appropriate way possible.

Consider this scenario: You are in Charleston, South Carolina, making a presentation to the traffic manager at a midsized manufacturing firm. She asks "Do you work with any carriers that go to Des Moines, Iowa?" The short—and honest—answer is that you do not. So rather than lie, you simply say "No, I'm sorry." And you've lost every ounce of sales momentum you've built to that point.

But suppose you respond to her question with a question of your own. You might say "Why do you ask?" or "Do you have shipments going to Des Moines?" If she says the reason for her question is that she ships a truckload a week to Des Moines, you can ask more questions about the move and her needs, and offer to get back with her after you've had a chance to find a carrier with a more competitive rate and service package than she has now. But if she says "No, we don't ship out there, but one of our senior managers just left us to take a job with a company there, so I was just thinking about that city," you can avoid a flat "no" answer and instead emphasize your flexibility and willingness to shop until you find what your customers want.

This is a technique you can apply to just about any situation and relationship. Suppose your spouse says "Are you hungry?" If you just say "yes," you might find yourself presented with a gourmet home-cooked meal—or being dragged out the door to a restaurant you didn't really want to go to. It's always better to know what's behind the question before you answer.

Steak or Sizzle

If you've ever taken a basic sales course, you've probably heard "sell the sizzle, not the steak." What that means is you need to understand the difference between features and benefits—and focus on the benefits.

A feature is an aspect of the service you provide; the benefit is what the customer gains from that aspect. For example, that you will call the shipper with delivery notification within two hours of the freight being unloaded is a feature. That the shipper has the peace of mind of knowing that the freight has been delivered on time and in good condition is a benefit. That you have access to thousands of carriers is a feature. That by using your firm, your customers are assured of getting the equipment they need when they need it is a benefit.

Before you ever call or visit a prospect for the first time, put together a presentation that includes needs-identification and benefits-selling, and practice it. Don't worry that you'll sound rehearsed; the reality is that the better you know your stuff, the more natural and confident you'll appear.

> **Bright Idea**
>
> Turn maintaining current customer records into a sales opportunity for your business. Call every customer at least once a year and say something like "We're checking our records for accuracy and completeness." Go through the information you have and then say "Do you have any needs we haven't discussed that we might be able to help you with?"

Does Anyone Object?

Another long-time sales training phrase is "handling objections." That sounds much more frightening than it really is.

In most professional sales situations, an "objection" comes in the form of a question, and whether it's a question or a statement, it is usually a request for more information.

For example, a prospective customer might say something like "How many carriers do you have agreements with?" or "I know you're new; I'm not sure you have the

▲

Inward Bound

Beyond talking to the traffic manager or the shipping department, you should also build a relationship with the purchasing department. As part of the terms of their agreements, many buyers have the right to select the mode and carrier. In many companies, the traffic department gets involved in routing these shipments, but there are still plenty of businesses where purchasing and traffic work independently. If you can make a purchasing agent's life easier by helping him find the most economical and efficient method of moving inbound freight, you'll have a steady stream of business.

experience I need." Both of these statements might be seen as objections, but what they really are is a chance for you to tell the prospect about the benefits he or she will gain by using you.

It's important to keep in mind that while freight may not appear particularly glamorous, for most companies, the efficient and timely movement of cargo is critical to their ongoing operations. Selecting a broker or carrier is not a decision most shippers make lightly or casually. You'll find your customers very much involved in both the sales process and in the ongoing service. You've chosen a highly interactive business, and you can expect your customers to view you and your staff as the service.

Ask For the Business

One of the most difficult parts of a sales call for most people is the close—but it shouldn't be. If you've been paying attention—if you identified your prospect's needs and determined that you can satisfy them, if you've focused on benefits rather than features—then asking the prospect to make that final commitment should be a natural evolution of the sales call.

Here's one approach that works well: Find out what internal procedure the customer would have to change to give you his or her business. This is a simple matter of asking: "If you were to decide to let us handle your next load to Phoenix, what would you have to do?" When the prospect answers the question—perhaps with something like "I'd have to tell the shipping clerk to call you"—ask if you can have the shipping clerk step in so you can answer any questions that person might have.

If the prospect resists, find out why. Say: "We've agreed that we have the services you need, that our rates are competitive, and we're in a position to provide some extras you're not getting now. Is there any reason why you shouldn't call the shipping clerk in now to give us a chance to prove ourselves on the next shipment?"

Prospects rarely say no without some sort of an explanation—an objection—that you'll have a chance to overcome. And even if you don't get the business—and you won't get it all—you'll at least know why.

Once you have devised your sales strategy, you'll be selling like a pro. Now you'll need some insights on financial management, the subject of the next chapter.

9

Financial Management

One of the great things about the freight broker business is that it doesn't require a tremendous amount of start-up cash to purchase facilities and equipment—you can be up and running with just a computer, fax machine, and phone—but it does require a substantial amount of cash or a significant credit line, virtually from day one. Precisely how much depends, of course, on your business volume, but you need to have sufficient cash on hand to pay your carriers on time, and that will likely be weeks before your shippers pay you.

This fact cannot be stressed enough: Cash flow management is critical in this business. If you don't pay your carriers on time, they'll stop accepting your loads. And though the industry is huge, in many ways, it is also like a small town—everybody knows everybody else's business. If you're not paying your bills on time, it won't be long before every carrier—and maybe even the shippers—find out about it. In a relationship business like freight brokering, a good reputation is essential, so protect yours by paying your bills on time.

You should monitor your cash flow constantly. Look at your receivables and payables on a daily basis. Cultivate fast-paying customers, and be sure your sales staff is explaining the need for prompt payment to new customers.

Successful brokers tend to take a conservative approach to financial management. "We don't do a lot of borrowing," says Bill Tucker in Cherry Hill, New Jersey. "We have a great credit rating and good cash flow, but we don't want to just borrow and expand for expansion's sake. We're focused on service. We have a fiduciary relationship and responsibility to our carriers and to anybody else we owe money to, and to our employees."

Ideally, you'll open your doors with enough cash in the bank to pay all your expenses and your carriers until revenue from your customers (shippers) starts coming in. More practically, you may need to look at short-term credit options, such as unsecured commercial bank loans, borrowing against your accounts receivable, or selling your accounts receivable (a process known as factoring, which is explained in more detail later in this chapter). You may have a tough time with conventional loan sources, because by traditional lending standards, most freight brokers would not be considered bankable. Even if you have a record of paying your bills on time, you will likely need a revolving line of credit significantly higher than whatever assets you have to offer for collateral.

Setting Credit Policies

Because you are billing your shippers, or sometimes the consignees, you need to set credit policies and procedures. When you extend credit, you do so under the assumption that the customer intends to pay, is capable of paying, and that nothing will prevent him or her from paying. Most of your customers will be honest and dependable when paying their bills, but that doesn't mean you should blindly extend credit without first gathering and verifying information.

Each new customer should complete a credit application, and you should check the information he or she provides. This is standard practice in business. If a customer

Tax Facts

You've probably heard this most of your life: The only two sure things in this world are death and taxes. Businesses—including freight brokers—are required to pay a wide range of taxes. Keep good records so you can offset your local, state, and federal income taxes with the expenses of operating your company. If you have employees, you'll be responsible for paying payroll taxes. If you operate as a corporation, you'll have to pay payroll taxes for yourself; as a sole proprietor, you'll pay self-employment tax. Then there are property taxes, taxes on your equipment and inventory (minimal though it may be), fees and taxes to maintain your corporate status, your business license fee (which is really a tax), and other lesser-known taxes. Take the time to review all your tax liabilities with your accountant, and check out the taxes section in *Start Your Own Business* for more information.

objects to completing a credit application, seriously consider whether extending credit to that customer is a safe thing to do. Look at it this way: When you extend credit for a service, you are essentially granting an unsecured, interest-free loan. Once the goods have been moved and delivered, you can't take back the service—and you (depending, of course, of the terms of your carrier agreement) are responsible for paying the carrier whether or not the shipper pays you.

Thanks in large part to the old Interstate Commerce Commission regulation that required payment of freight bills within seven days, most shippers have systems set up to pay freight bills faster than other invoices. "In the old days, it was regulation," Tucker says. "Today, it's entirely contractual among the parties. But carriers usually have pretty narrow margins. [Trucking companies have] a serious financial burden to carry. [They have] to pay the driver, buy the fuel, buy the insurance, and make the loan payments on the equipment—all before the driver goes out the door." Cooperative shippers understand the economic realities of trucking, and that if truckers are going to stay in business, they must be paid promptly. But you will still have customers who will take as long as you allow them to pay. It's your responsibility to set your terms and make those terms very clear to your customers.

You can include your terms (essentially when payment is due) on your credit application and have customers sign an acknowledgment that they know, understand, and agree to abide by your policies. On each invoice, clearly indicate the date the invoice will become past due.

Warning Signs

Just because a customer passed your first credit check with flying colors, don't neglect to re-evaluate his or her credit status—in fact, you should do it on a regular basis.

Tell customers when you initially grant their credit applications that you have a policy of periodically reviewing accounts so that when you do it, it's not a surprise. Things can change very quickly in the business world, and a company that is on sound financial footing this year may be quite wobbly next year.

An annual re-evaluation of all customers on open account is a good idea—but if you start to see trouble in the interim, don't wait to take action. Another time to re-evaluate a customer's credit is when they request an increase in their credit line.

Some key trouble signs are a slowdown in payments, increased complaints, and difficulty getting answers to your payment inquiries. Even a sharp increase in volume could signal trouble; companies concerned that they may lose their credit privileges with you may try to milk you while they can, and if they aren't paying other brokers or carriers, they may have already lost some credit privileges and be looking to replace those sources. Pay attention to what your customers are doing; a major change in their customer base or product lines is something you may want to monitor.

Tucker says the process of providing good service to customers will also alert you to potential credit problems. "Just in the course of my relationship with the company, I talk to the president, I talk to the salespeople, I talk to the manufacturing people, I talk to the traffic manager, and even the guy who loads the trucks," he says. Changes in a company's transportation needs and patterns can be early indicators of a problem.

So what does Tucker do if he spots a red flag? "It depends on the details and on how serious it is. We may be [able to] help them solve their financial or market problem. But you also have to keep at arm's length if they are getting into trouble. You have to either quietly be 'running out of trucks,' or tell them the salesperson will be in there every Friday to pick up a check. It's our job to protect the money every way we can, including refusing to extend more credit and walking away from the business. Sometimes you just have to do that. But you have to know when, and you have to be able to evaluate those things. And we stay close enough to the customer so we can at least minimize the hit."

Most customers accept routine credit reviews as a sound business practice. A customer who objects may well have something to hide—and that's something you need to know.

Cash Flow Controls

Certainly cash flow is important to any business, but it is critical to a freight brokerage. You need to keep sufficient cash on hand to pay your regular operating expenses and your carriers, but not so much that you miss out on revenue from alternative investments. In addition, you need to take steps to protect your company from internal theft.

Before you hire your first employee, set up internal controls to safeguard your assets and assure maximum cash flow management. One such control is to require proper authorization of transactions. Be specific as to which individuals are authorized to carry out what tasks, and hold them accountable for their actions.

You'll also want to establish a separation of duties so the person responsible for custody of an asset is not also responsible for record-keeping for that same asset. This prevents someone from stealing and then changing records to cover up what he or she has done.

Smart Tip

Often, employees are motivated to steal by the feeling that they are being underpaid or that the business owner is making excessive profits on workers' efforts, so the employee feels "entitled" to steal. Help prevent this attitude by paying fair wages and treating your employees with respect.

Be sure the records you keep are adequate to satisfy financial and tax reporting requirements, as well as the federal regulations governing freight brokers. However, you should limit access to both assets and documents to prevent unauthorized use or theft; keep access on a needs-only basis.

Finally, set up a system to independently verify individual performance. Someone who was not involved in the work should check it for accuracy. This will help uncover intentional theft and fraud, as well as unintentional errors.

Beyond techniques to protect your assets, you'll also need systems to maximize them. Consider these:

- *Set up a sweep account.* This is a service banks offer that lets you earn the maximum interest on all the money in your accounts, even if it's just overnight, without penalties or concerns of bouncing checks. The system is set up so funds are automatically moved—or swept—in and out of the appropriate accounts each day. If your banker is reluctant to set you up with this type of an account, shop around for one who will.

- *Use a lockbox for receivables.* Another bank service, a lockbox, works like this: Your customers mail their payments to a post office box that your bank rents in your company's name. The bank sends a courier several times a day to clear out the box, checks are immediately deposited into your account—literally within hours of their arrival in the mail—and you get a report outlining all the transactions in as much detail as you want, as frequently as you want. Lockboxes mean you no longer have to run to the bank with deposits, or spend your (or one of your staff member's) valuable time opening envelopes, recording payments and preparing deposits.

- *Accept electronic payments.* Talk to your banker about getting set up so you can accept payments through electronic transfers.

- *Invoice on a timely basis.* You can't expect customers to pay until you've issued an invoice, so get your invoices out as soon as you know what all the appropriate charges on a given shipment are. Be sure you include whatever documentation is necessary (copies of bills of lading, delivery receipts, etc.) for your customers to pay promptly.

- *Enforce your payment terms.* Be prepared to follow up on late bills as soon as they become past due. Initial reminders don't have to be ugly or obnoxious, but you want to make it clear that you expect your customers to pay by the terms to which they agreed when they applied for credit.

> **⚠ Beware!**
> Mail thieves operate even in the nicest of neighborhoods, both residential and commercial. If you do not have a secure, locked mailbox, and you receive checks by mail, rent a post office box so you know they'll be safe.

The Power of Compensating Balances

One of the ways to measure the value of a company is its profitability. When it comes to the value of a company to a banker, the measure is in compensating balances. Though your ultimate net profit may be pennies on each revenue dollar, you are still funneling large sums of cash through your bank account as you collect from shippers and pay carriers.

Banks are very interested in companies with large amounts of cash flow. Even though the money doesn't really belong to you, you have temporary control over it. It will spend a certain amount of time in your account, and that time can be very important to a bank.

As you build your relationship with your banker, be sure to point out how much cash you expect to move through your accounts—it's called compensating balances— and ask what types of services and/or concessions the bank can provide you because of it.

Managing Payables

Due to the nature of the industry, paying carriers on time is critical. In fact, Bill Tucker says you are a financier of sorts for the carriers you use, because you'll likely be paying them before you get paid by your shippers.

While carriers make up the major portion of your payables, you have other bills to pay. Certainly on-time payment of all your bills is essential to building a good credit rating and maintaining a good reputation. But by the same token, it is not good cash management to pay your bills before they are due. If your suppliers are willing to extend terms of net 30, then it's OK for you to take 30 days to pay that bill—it's not necessary to pay it 10 or 15 days early. Keep your money working for you in your accounts for as long as possible.

Facts on Factoring

Factoring is the sale of accounts receivable to a third-party funding source for immediate cash. In a typical factoring arrangement, the client (you) makes a sale, delivers the product or service to the customer, and generates an invoice. The factor (the funding source) purchases the right to collect on that invoice by agreeing to pay the client the face value of the invoice less a discount, typically 2 to 6 percent. The factor pays 75 to 80 percent of the face value immediately and forwards the remainder, less the discount, when the customer pays.

Beware!
As a broker, you'll collect and disperse a tremendous amount of cash. Resist the temptation to spend money that is already obligated to payables. "If they're not good money managers, that's where a lot of the start-up brokerage operations get into trouble," says Indianapolis freight broker Chuck Andrews. "They see all this money and start spending it. Then it comes time to pay the bills, and there are no funds."

Because factors are not extending credit to their clients, but instead to their clients' customers, they are more concerned about the customers' ability to pay rather than the financial status of their clients. That means a company with creditworthy customers may be able to factor even though it couldn't qualify for a traditional loan.

Though the principles are the same, factors vary based on the type of businesses they handle, the amounts of invoices they purchase, and the specific services they provide. Choosing a factor is like choosing a bank—you have to find the right match.

Though factoring is almost as old as commerce itself, it was used primarily by very large corporations until the mid-1980s. Since then, awareness of factoring has grown, and more companies are incorporating this weapon into their cash management arsenal. Even so, there are still plenty of misconceptions about factoring.

Though factoring is often confused with accounts receivable financing, it's important to understand that this is not a loan, and it does not create a liability on your balance sheet. Rather, it is the sale of an asset, which in this case is an invoice for goods or services received by the customer.

Factoring is also considered one of the most expensive forms of financing, and while it may appear so at first glance, that's not necessarily true. The factor's fee is generally higher than the interest rate a traditional lender charges, but you need to also consider that factors provide a wide range of services that banks do not. They can help with credit checks, take over a significant portion of the accounting function for you, and generate reports to help you track your financial status.

Once you get a handle on money matters, you should be well on your way to running a successful freight brokerage. Good luck!

Beware!

Indianapolis freight broker Chuck Andrews offers this word of caution on factoring: You need to watch your commission levels because if you are in a highly competitive area and working on margins that are less than the industry average, you may end up operating at a loss if you try to factor.

Tales from the
Trenches

By now, you should know how to get started
and have a good idea of what to do—and not do—in your own
freight brokerage. But nothing teaches as well as the voice of
experience. So we asked established freight brokers what has
contributed to their success and what they think causes companies to fail. Here's what they told us:

Use Advertising and
Marketing Techniques that Work

Track your marketing efforts so you can concentrate on the techniques that work and eliminate the ones that don't.

Smyrna, Tennessee, freight broker Cathy Davis said small giveaway items, such as pens, note pads, caps, and T-shirts, work well. Company newsletters with personal and industry information also get a good response. She said donations to fundraising events may be helpful (depending on the event and the degree to which it's promoted), but the impact of web site sponsorships is questionable. She recommended developing a three-panel printed brochure that is easy to include with letters, invoices, and checks.

Chuck Andrews, the Indianapolis freight broker, builds name recognition by placing periodic ads in association newsletters as well as in annual association and industry directories.

Prepare for the Future

Certainly it's understandable that at this point, your primary focus is getting started, but you also need to think about the future. Develop a succession plan that is reviewed and revised annually. Know how leadership will be transferred when it becomes necessary—either through voluntary or involuntary departures.

Don't Reinvent the Wheel

Look around for good ideas and good products that people are already using that you can incorporate into your operation. Everything you do doesn't have to be original; get ideas from other brokers, carriers, shippers, and even totally unrelated businesses.

Bloomingdale, Illinois, freight broker Ron Williamson learned this the hard way when he hired someone to develop a proprietary computer system. "That was a mistake because it was not a totally integrated system that would save us time and make us more efficient," he recalls. "Later on, we found a packaged program that had all the bells and whistles we needed."

Get Rid of Carriers
that Don't Perform

Every trucking company will have an occasional service problem, but when the service failures become chronic, drop the carrier from your roster. "You won't keep your customers very long if you're having constant problems with your carriers," says

Ron Williamson. Of course, he acknowledges that in the beginning you probably won't know who all the good and bad carriers are. While it's one thing to be understanding and give a carrier a second chance, you need to draw the line before the problems affect your own business.

Maintain a Broad and Diverse Customer Base

You need enough customers so that losing one—or even several—is not devastating. One of the biggest mistakes Cathy Davis ever made when she ran her freight brokerage was allowing one customer to control too much of her company's revenue. When that customer pulled away with very little notice, she was left scrambling to replace that business.

Get in the Spotlight

Because the freight industry is such a strongly relationship- and reputation-based business, it helps to put yourself in the public eye in a positive way as often as you can. Cathy Davis saw a favorable impact on her business from being the recipient of awards and by getting bylined articles published in trade publications.

Be Open to Evolution

Though a freight brokerage is extremely lucrative on its own, it's also a business that can lead to the development of other transportation-related operations, from consulting to buying trucks and being a carrier. Cherry Hill, New Jersey, freight broker Bill Tucker, for example, offers a wide range of logistics services.

Chuck Andrews started as a broker and then created his own separate trucking company to handle moves where the carriers he was using were short on equipment. Ron Williamson also started as a broker and has since created two trucking operations.

Protect Your Reputation

"Focus on building the highest-quality reputation you possibly can," advises Bill Tucker. "When a shortcut presents itself, but it's a little on the shady side, have the fortitude to pass it by, no matter how big the opportunity may seem. There are so many people in this industry who need good, solid, honest, reputable service—and long term, that's where the big money is. You survive, and you won't have a lot of doors closing to you because some bad story got out."

Bill Tucker compares the industry to a small village. "Everybody knows everybody else's business. It's amazing how fast word travels. Nothing will put you out of business or limit your success faster than the story of one bad transaction or one nasty court loss because of bad practices getting out into the marketplace. You're going to have to sweat for a while, pull your belt in once in a while, and [endure] some tough times. But do it the right way every time, don't take any shortcuts, provide high-quality service, and maintain your integrity, and you'll always have customers willing to pay a fair price and good carriers that want to work with you."

Appendix

They say you can never be rich enough or thin enough. While these could be argued, we say you can never have enough resources. Therefore, we present for your consideration a wealth of resources for you to check into, check out, and harness as part of your own personal information blitz.

Freight Broker Resources

These resources are intended to get you started on your research. They are by no means the only ones out there. We have done our research, but businesses—like those expired mailing list nixies—do tend to move, change, fold, and expand. As we have repeatedly stressed, do your homework. Get out there and do some investigating.

The best place to start? If you haven't yet joined the internet age, do it! Surfing the net is like waltzing through the fabled Library at Alexandria, with a breathtaking array of resources literally at your fingertips.

Associations and Regulatory Agencies

American Society of Transportation & Logistics (AST&L)
1700 N. Moore St., #1900, Arlington, VA 22209
(703) 524-5011, fax: (703) 524-5017
www.astl.org

American Trucking Association
2200 Mill Rd., Alexandria, VA 22314
(888) 333-1759
www.trucking.org

Delta Nu Alpha
An international transportation organization with a focus on education
1451 Elm Hill Pike, #205, Nashville, TN 37210
(866) 453-3662, (615) 360-6863
fax: (615) 360-1891
www.deltanualpha.org

Federal Highway Administration
400 7th St. SW, Washington, DC 20590
(202) 366-0650
www.fhwa.dot.gov

National Association of Small Trucking Companies
104 Stuart Dr., Hendersonville, TN 37075
(800) 264-8580, (615) 451-4555
fax: (615) 451-0041
www.nastc.com

National Association of Women Business Owners
(800) 556-2926, (703) 506-3268
www.nawbo.org

National Industrial Transportation League
1700 N. Moore St., #1900, Arlington, VA 22209-1904
(703) 524-5011, fax: (703) 524-5017
www.nitl.org

Surface Transportation Board (STB)
www.stb.dot.gov

Transportation Clubs International
A network of more than 200 local transportation organizations

P.O. Box 2223, Ocean Shores, WA 98569
(877) 858-8627
www.transportationclubsinternational.com

Transportation Intermediaries Association

An organization for North American transportation intermediaries, including property (freight) brokers, domestic freight forwarders, consolidators, ocean and air forwarders, intermodal marketing companies, perishable commodity brokers, logistics management firms, and motor carriers.
1625 Prince St., #200, Alexandria, VA 22314
(703) 299-5700, fax: (703) 836-0123
e-mail: info@tianet.org
www.tianet.org

Truckload Carriers Association

2200 Mill Rd., Alexandria, VA 22314
(703) 838-1950, fax: (703) 836-6610
www.truckload.org

U.S. Department of Transportation

www.dot.gov

Online Services and Resources

CompuNet Credit Services Inc.

P.O. Box 710, Lake Havasu City, AZ 86405
(888) 269-2237, (928) 680-9449
fax: (928) 680-4382
www.compunetcredit.com

getloaded.com

Online freight-matching service and other broker resources.
One Park West Cir., #300, Midlothian, VA 23114
(804) 744-6354, fax: (804) 744-8394
www.getloaded.com

Internet Truckstop

Online freight-matching service, credit reports, and more.
(800) 203-2540
www.truckstop.com

NetTrans

Online freight-matching service.

▲

(800) 209-2433, fax: (770) 209-7085
www.nettrans.com

Red Book Credit Services
10901 W. 84th Terr., Lenexa, KS 66214
(800) 252-1925, (913) 438-0606
fax: (913) 438-0690
www.rbcs.com

TransCore Commercial Services
Load-matching services, software, and other products and services.
11000 S.W. Stratus St., #100, Beaverton, OR 97008
(800) 547-5417, (503) 643-4331
fax: (503) 526-6453
www.transportationsoftware.com

Publications and Training Resources

Certified Transportation Broker
Offered by Transportation Intermediaries Association
1625 Prince St., #200, Alexandria, VA 22314
(703) 299-5700, fax: (703) 836-0123
e-mail: info@tianet.org
www.tianet.org

Leonard's Guides
Publishers of Motor Freight Directory, International Postal, Parcel & Cargo
Directory, National Warehouse & Distribution Directory, National Third Party
Logistics Directory, National Contract Carriers Directory, rate and mileage guides
and software.
49 E. Huntington Dr., Arcadia, CA 91006
(800) 574-5250
www.leonardsguide.com

New Broker Kit
Offered by Transportation Intermediaries Association, includes training materials,
sample contracts, and forms, FHWA registration information.
1625 Prince St., #200, Alexandria, VA 22314
(703) 299-5700, fax: (703) 836-0123
e-mail: info@tianet.org
www.tianet.org

Thomas Register of American Manufacturers
Thomas Publishing Company
5 Penn Plaza, New York, NY 10001
(212) 290-7277
www.thomasregister.com

Traffic World Magazine
1270 National Press Bldg., Washington, DC 20045
(202) 355-1150
www.trafficworld.com

Transport Topics
2200 Mill Rd., Alexandria, VA 22314
(703) 838-1770
www.ttnews.com

Software Creative Systems Corp.
Transportation software.
455 Frontage Rd., Burr Ridge, IL 60527
(630) 323-9099, fax: (630) 920-0384
www.csclink.com

Wolf Byte Software
5805 Whittle Rd., #208, Mississauga, ON L4Z 2J1 CAN
(888) 965-3298
www.wolfbytesoftware.com

Successful Freight Brokers
MCD Transportation Inc.
Donna J. Wood, CTB, President
Dionne R. Kegley, CTB, Vice President
1370 Hazelwood Dr., #201, Smyrna, TN 37167
(615) 459-5343, fax: (615) 459-3353
e-mail: mcd@mcdtrans.com
www.mcdtrans.com

Midwest Freight Brokers Inc.
Chuck Andrews
920 N. Shadeland Ave., Ste. 2A, Indianapolis, IN 46219
(317) 322-0758, fax (317) 322-0332
e-mail: mwfbho@aol.com
www.midwestfreightbrokers.com

▲

RJW Logistics Inc.
Ronald Williamson, CTB
P.O. Box 700, Bloomingdale, IL 60108
(630) 424-2400, fax: (630) 545-0051
www.rjwgroup.com

Transportation Resources Inc.
Joseph E. Workman
P.O. Box 4120, Winter Park, FL 32793
(407) 831-0700, fax: (407) 831-8006
www.tranco.org

Tucker Co.
William J. Tucker
900 Dudley Ave., Cherry Hill, NJ 08002
(800) 229-7780, (856) 317-9600
fax: (856) 317-9699
www.tuckerco.com

Glossary

Accessorial charges: charges assessed by a carrier for services provided in addition to basic transportation, such as extra pickups, loading, and unloading.

Air-ride: trailers built to reduce road shock and designed to carry fragile items; the suspension system supports the load on air-filled rubber bags rather than steel springs.

Backhaul: the return trip of a vehicle from the destination back to the origin.

Bill of lading: a document that serves as the contract of carriage between the shipper and the carrier.

Bobtail: a tractor operating without a trailer.

Bracing: securing items inside a vehicle to prevent damage.

Break-bulk: the separation of a load into smaller shipments for delivery to ultimate consignees.

Claim: a charge made against a carrier for loss, damage or overcharge.

Class rate: a rate constructed from a classification and a uniform distance system.

Commercial zone: the area surrounding a city or town to which rates quoted for that city or town also apply.

Common carrier: any person or agency publicly engaged in the business of transporting passengers or freight; common carriers are subject to two stringent obligations: compulsory service and liability for loss or damage to goods.

Consignee: the receiver of a freight shipment, usually the buyer.

Consignor: the sender of a freight shipment, usually the seller.

Consolidation: the collection of smaller shipments to form a larger quantity to get lower transportation rates.

Container (shipping container): standard-sized rectangular box used to transport freight by ship, rail, or motor carrier.

Contract carrier: a company that transports freight under contract with one shipper or a limited number of shippers.

Cost per hundred weight (cwt): an amount charged per hundred pounds of freight.

Density: a physical characteristic of a commodity, which is important in rate-making since density affects vehicle utilization; determining density requires measuring its mass per unit per volume, or pounds per foot.

Detention: the charge assessed by the carrier when the shipper or receiver holds a truck or trailer beyond the time allowed for loading and unloading.

Doubles (twins, twin trailers): a tractor and two semitrailers that are connected.

Drayage: a motor carrier that operates locally, providing pickup and delivery service.

Driver assist: when a driver is asked to assist in the loading or unloading process; sometimes treated as an extra charge on a per-hour or flat rate.

Driver's log sheets: a log of miles traveled, hours of driving, off-times, and rest periods that drivers are required to keep.

Dry van: a nonrefrigerated, noninsulated semitrailer handling general commodity freight that can withstand outside temperatures without suffering damage.

Empty backhaul: when a truck returns empty from the destination to the point of origin and therefore does not generate return-trip revenue.

Exclusive use: a request made by shippers that means their freight is the only freight on the truck.

Exempt carrier: a for-hire carrier that is exempt from economic regulations.

Expediting: determining where a shipment is during transit and attempting to speed up its delivery; many big companies have expeditors on staff who do this full time.

Flats (or flatbeds): a flat, solidly built trailer designed to handle heavier and bulkier loads than a dry van, such as metal, equipment, and machinery.

FOB: a term of sale that defines who is to pay transportation charges for a shipment, who is to control the movement of the shipment, or where title to the goods passes from the seller to the buyer; originally an acronym for "free on board."

For-hire carrier: a company that provides truck transportation of cargo belonging to others and is paid for doing so.

Freight bill: the carrier's invoice for transportation charges for a particular shipment.

Freight broker: the middle person who connects shippers and carriers.

Freight payable: technically, a freight bill that needs to be paid; in common use, it also refers to the special payables department large shippers may have that is dedicated to paying freight bills.

Freight pool: a collection of trailer loads waiting for assignment to a driver and tractor.

Front haul: the initial movement of the vehicle from the origin to the destination.

Full truckload (FTL): a shipment occupying the entire trailer, typically with a weight of 30,000 pounds or more.

Gross weight: the total weight of the goods being shipped, including packing and packaging materials.

Hazmat: Hazardous materials, as classified by the U.S. Environmental Protection Agency (EPA); transportation of hazardous materials is strictly regulated by the U.S. Department of Transportation.

Incentive rate: a rate designed to encourage shippers to ship heavier volumes per shipment.

Interline: two or more motor carriers working together to haul a shipment.

Intermodal: combining two or more modes of transportation, such as truck and rail, truck and air, or rail and ocean.

Interstate Commerce Commission (ICC): a federal regulatory agency that was abolished in 1995.

Joint rate: a rate over a route that involves two or more carriers transporting the shipment.

Just-in-time (JIT) inventory management: an inventory management technique designed to reduce inventory levels by delivering parts just as they are needed on the production line.

Layover: a delay preventing a driver from unloading as scheduled at destination; some carriers charge an additional fee for this.

Less-than-truckload (LTL): a shipment occupying less than the entire trailer, typically with a weight of less than 30,000 pounds; it can be combined with other shipments to make up a full truckload.

Less-than-truckload (LTL) carrier: a trucking company that consolidates less-than-truckload cargo for multiple destinations on one vehicle.

Motor carrier (MC): a company that provides truck transportation.

Multiple drops: a delivery requiring more than one stop.

Net weight: the weight of the goods being shipped, excluding the packaging and packing materials.

OS&D: an acronym for "over, short and damaged."

Over (overage): when the piece count of a shipment is more than what is indicated on the bill of lading.

Over-the-road: a motor carrier operation that reflects long-distance, intercity moves; the opposite of local operations.

Owner-operator: a trucker who owns and operates his own truck(s).

P&D: pickup and delivery.

Pallet: a movable platform, usually made of wood, for the storage or transportation of goods.

Pallet exchange: the process of replacing a shipper's pallets, leaving an equitable number of empty pallets when picking up goods loaded on pallets, then picking up a comparable number of empty pallets from the consignee when the freight is delivered.

Payload: the weight of the cargo being hauled.

Peddle run: a truck route with frequent delivery stops.

Private carrier: a carrier that provides transportation service of its own cargo to the firm that owns or leases the vehicles and does not charge a fee.

Process agent: a representative upon whom court papers may be served in any proceeding brought against a motor carrier, broker, or freight forwarder; freight brokers are required to list with the FHWA the names of process agents in each state in which they have an office, and in which they write contracts.

Product (pro), load and invoice numbers: numbers assigned to shipments for identification purposes.

Pup trailer: short semitrailer, usually between 26 and 32 feet long, with a single axle; often used as doubles or triples.

Purchase order number: a number that buyers assign to their purchase orders that shippers will usually include on their freight documents so consignees can easily identify the load when it is delivered.

Ragtop: a box-like trailer open at the top, on which a large canvas is spread to protect cargo from the elements; primarily used for large, bulky bales or boxes, loose materials and sometimes for nursery stock shipments.

Reasonable rate: a rate high enough to cover the carrier's costs but not so high that it enables the carrier to realize monopolistic profits.

Reefer: a refrigerated, insulated semitrailer.

Round trip: when a driver moves a load to a specific point, reloads at the point, and returns to the original point of pickup.

Semitrailer: a truck trailer supported at the rear by its own wheels and at the front by a fifth wheel mounted to a tractor or dolly.

Shipper order number: a number assigned to a load or shipment by the shipper for tracking purposes; this number should be referred to on invoices and any other documents concerning the shipment.

Shipping container: see container.

Shipping weight: the gross weight of a shipment, including product, packaging, and packing materials.

Short (shortage): when the piece count of a shipment is less than indicated on the bill of lading.

Short-haul discrimination: charging more for a shorter haul than a longer haul over the same route, in the same direction, and for the same commodity; this is an accepted industry practice since certain fixed costs apply no matter how long the trip is

Skid: a pallet.

Split pickup: a pickup requiring more than one stop.

▲

Tanker: a trailer shaped like a huge tank designed to handle liquid and loose, fine bulk materials.

Tariff: a publication that contains a carrier's rates, accessorial charges, and rules.

Tend to load: when the drivers attend to the loading and unloading of their trailers.

Truckload (TL) carrier: a trucking company which dedicates trailers to a single shipper's cargo, as opposed to an LTL (less than truckload) carrier which transports the consolidated cargo of several shippers and makes multiple deliveries.

Trailer on flatcar (TOFC): a method of moving cargo that involves transporting semitrailers on railroad flatcars.

Ton mile taxes: taxes based on the weight (tonnage) of the shipment and the number of miles it travels (tax per ton, per mile).

Tracing: determining where a shipment is during the course of the move.

Tractor: a truck designed primarily to pull a semitrailer by means of a fifth wheel mounted over the rear axle(s); sometimes called a truck tractor or highway tractor to differentiate it from a farm tractor.

Tractor trailer: a tractor and semitrailer combination.

Traffic management: the management of the various activities associated with buying and controlling transportation services for a shipper or consignee or both.

Transit time: the total time that elapses from pickup to delivery of a shipment.

Trip leasing: leasing a company's vehicle to another transportation provider for a single trip.

Truckload (TL): the quantity of freight required to fill a trailer, usually over 10,000 pounds.

Weight per case: the total, or gross, weight per case, carton, or box.

Index

The world has changed

Shouldn't Your Retirement Strategy Follow Suit?

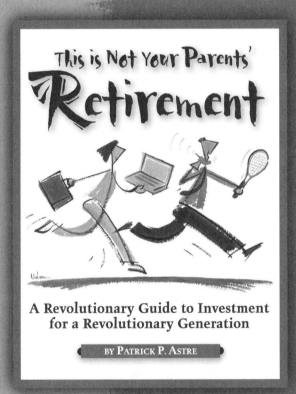

This is Not Your Parents' Retirement

A Revolutionary Guide to Investment for a Revolutionary Generation

BY PATRICK P. ASTRE

You're destined for a longer, more active retirement than any generation before you— and you want the cash to do it in style. Forget nest eggs. There's a revolution afoot in retirement planning, and expert Patrick Astre divulges the investment secrets that create multiple income streams for life.

"This is absolutely a must-have book for anyone reaching for financial independence."
-Lynn Parrott, vice president
John Hancock/Manulife Financial

"This is one of the best financial books I have read. It's clear, easy to understand and a great guide for anyone who wants to build and preserve wealth toward retirement."
-Arnie Pechler, vice president,
Farmers & Traders Life

Online updates at www.thisisnot yourparents retirement.com

Pick up your copy today!

AVAILABLE AT ALL FINE BOOKSTORES AND ONLINE BOOKSELLERS
WWW.ENTREPRENEURPRESS.COM

Entrepreneur. Press

WITHDRAWAL